# VACCINES ON TRIAL

Truths and Consequences

Pierre St. Clair

Copyright © Pierre St. Clair 2017

All Rights Reserved

This book is copyright protected. No part of this book may be reproduced in any form or by any means including information storage and retrieval systems, except in the case of brief quotations, without prior written consent from the author.

All legal, medical, and historical references herein are quoted from transcripts of court documents, news media, attorneys, doctors, documentaries, and industry insiders from their public statements, interviews, books, or papers. No copyright infringement is intended or projected.

Readers acknowledge that the author is not rendering medical, financial, legal, or professional advice of any kind. The information contained herein is for educational purposes only and is not intended to diagnose, or recommend treatment for any adverse vaccine disorders.

Every attempt has been made to provide accurate, up-to-date, reliable, and complete information. The author or publisher is not responsible for losses, direct or indirect, which may be incurred as a result of using the information contained herein, including, but not limited to, errors, omissions, or inaccuracies.

Due to the dynamic nature of the internet, web addresses or links found in this book may have changed or may no longer be valid.

# DEDICATION

All blessings to the children who suffered
due to adverse vaccine reactions.

All blessings to the parents who stood by
in good and bad times to give affection,
support, and assistance through all
the challenges and complications.

# Contents

Preface .................................................................. 1
Introduction ......................................................... 5
1: Vaccine Verification ..................................... 23
2: Herd Immunity ............................................. 37
3: Undeniable Facts .......................................... 65
4: Mandatory Vaccination ................................ 87
5: 20th Century Vaccine Law .......................... 103
6: Childhood Vaccine Injury Act .................... 115
7: Unavoidably Unsafe .................................... 131
8: Supreme Court Fallout ................................ 149
9: Foregoing Vaccines ..................................... 161
10: Rage Against the Machine ......................... 183
11: No Right of Refusal ................................... 199
12: Healthy People 2020 .................................. 217
13: The Big Pharma Lobby .............................. 235
14: What's in Those Vaccines .......................... 241
15: The Future of Vaccines ............................. 271
16: Appendix .................................................... 285
17: CDC Excipient Table ................................. 305
   Acknowledgements ..................................... 325

# REVIEWS

Thorough and comprehensive guide to many issues facing parents and guardians.

– Vitality Matters, LLC

Provides many facts for helping parents educate themselves fully on vaccination issues.

– Kathryn Blades

Very thorough research to make sure nothing important was left out.

– Ron P. Marinelli

# PREFACE

**Mandatory shots or freedom to choose?**

Mandatory vaccination is sweeping across North America, Europe, Australia and New Zealand. Parental rights to informed consent before medical intervention of their children is being revoked.

Pediatricians assure us that adverse vaccine reactions are rare, and parents accept this assurance based on faith in doctors, health care providers, and government officials who say vaccines have saved millions of lives.

Yet the Association of American Physicians and Surgeons (AAPS) disputes this assurance.

In their Fact Sheet on Mandatory Vaccinations, April 9/2009, they note: "The CDC admits that the reported number of adverse effects of vaccines is probably only 10% of actual adverse effects."

After exhaustively examining many vaccine studies, the U.S. Supreme Court ruled in Bruesewitz v. Wyeth 2011 that: "Vaccines are unavoidably unsafe and there shall be no more lawsuits against any vaccine company."

Moreover, the AAPS doesn't favor mandatory vaccines as stated in their Fact Sheet that they "attempted to halt government or school districts from blanket vaccine mandates that violate parental Informed Consent."

## Studies by leading healthcare scientists

This book documents many issues regarding vaccines that are not clearly explained or even revealed to the public. The studies and testimonies of leading healthcare officials provide a darker perspective of vaccine efficacy.

The information revealed here will be an eye-opener for parents who naively accepted assurances from doctors, the medical industry, pharmaceutical companies, and even local government about the safety of vaccines.

Scientific studies in the U.S, Germany, Sweden, and New Zealand comparing vaccinated and unvaccinated children show unvaccinated kids to be healthier than their vaccinated peers.

Charts and graphs on countries that increase the number of shots rank the U.S. 34th for infant mortality among first world nations.

The book, *Critical Vaccine Studies*, lists 400 case studies that show vaccinated kids have more health problems later in life.

Preface

## Vaccine Ingredients

The MMR vaccine has human DNA from aborted fetuses, listed as WI-38 by the CDC.

MMR also has DNA material from chicken and cow embryos.

Many vaccines contain mercury, aluminum, formaldehyde, polysorbate 80 and other chemicals unfamiliar to most parents.

Chapter Seventeen lists every ingredient in every vaccine that is itemized by the CDC on their website cdc.gov.

You can find out how these chemicals affect the human body and why they are used in vaccines by searching online with Google.

## How many shots is too many?

Before 1970, American kids were fully vaccinated with 2 shots. By 1986, it was 10 shots.

Today, kids have to get 24 shots before the age of two.

That's one shot/month of foreign DNA injected into a baby's tiny developing body. It's unprecedented in human history.

## The internet transformed the landscape

In the 20th century almost everyone was pro-vaccine. But pro-vax parents became anti-vax when their children experienced harmful side-effects.

American families gradually discovered hundreds of thousands of vaccine-injured children. This discovery led to anti-vaccine attitudes. The modern anti-vax movement began when outraged parents became warriors to protect children harmed by vaccines.

These mothers are now well-informed about adverse side-effects. They have researched how aluminum and mercury in modern vaccines are toxic to a baby's developing body. They have understood the results of 240 studies published on PubMed.

Today, adverse vaccine reactions are not rare at all. You can chat online with mothers of vaccine-injured kids, read books about toddlers harmed by vaccines, and watch films documenting how autism appears after vaccination, not before.

## Do benefits outweigh risks?

Benefits have never harmed children. That's why this book documents vaccine risks. Informed consent recognizes citizen's democratic right to choose.

Parents do have a legal right to avoid potential risk to their children from unwanted medical intervention.

## Preface

This book investigates vaccines from the medical perspective, legal perspective, scientific perspective, business perspective. ethical perspective, historical perspective, parent's perspective, and the child's perspective.

Mandatory vaccines is a far more complex issue than simple pro-vax and anti-vax labels that some people portray with petty, stereotyped, black-and-white rhetoric.

Informed persons do not frame the vaccine issue with such polarizing terms that cause strife between families with opposite views.

Please look at the scientific studies referenced here to decide the issues for yourself. Every insight, insider tip, and jewel of wisdom is organized into a broad anthology. Learn lessons that may save years of heartbreak, and thousands on hospital bills.

The intent is to provide a comprehensive guide for families wanting to make informed decisions before vaccinating their children. It's a complete handbook on the wisdom, experience, and approval of many respected medical experts. Most parents aren't against vaccines, they're against being forced.

If you believe in mandatory vaccination, and refuse to have your children play with unvaccinated kids, this book is not for you.

For people who are open to examine the latest scientific studies and statistics, this book offers valuable research not available to the public.

**Mandatory vaccines or freedom to choose?**

That is the issue discussed in this book. Whether it's more noble to suffer our fate, allow our children to be vaccinated against our will, and accept that there may be adverse reactions; or to stand strong, demand informed consent, and oppose mandatory vaccination in defense of our lawful claim as responsible citizens to stop the denial of parental rights.

We have to take a stand for the democratic right to make our own choices in a free society.

# INTRODUCTION

*The day we see the truth and cease to speak
is the day we begin to die.*

- Martin Luther King, Jr.

Among the unsettling considerations today is whether to vaccinate your child, or to forego vaccination.

Never before have so many vaccines been injected into American infants. According to statistics at the Centers for Disease Control and Prevention (CDC) over 10 million shots are given to kids yearly.

This book will examine every aspect of vaccination; the good, the bad, and of course, the ugly. Every parent should be well versed on the difference between vaccination and immunization.

Vaccination is temporary because it needs booster shots to remain effective; immunization is lifelong. Vaccination also means that "unknown substances" will be injected into American infants twenty-four times before the age of two.

I have listed all these bizarre ingredients for every vaccine in Chapter Seventeen. The list comes from the CDC Excipient Table published on cdc.gov.

Any person over 45 can verify that they were considered fully protected with only two or three shots. What has happened today is that youngsters are required, and even forced, to have multiple vaccinations before they're allowed to receive an education.

Of course, an unvaccinated child may contract a disease that could cause unnecessary suffering. That's a tragedy. Other parents will consider a decision to forego vaccination unwise or even immoral.

Conversely, vaccines have caused severe side-effects in children. Adverse reactions can lead to debilitating symptoms or even premature death; for example SIDS (sudden infant death syndrome). It's an outcome that leaves a horrifying and lasting shock on parents, resulting in years of regret and guilt. That's another tragedy.

In many cases kids appear fine after vaccination. But the focus of this book is the frequent cases in which children became impaired after vaccination, either within days, weeks, or longer.

Doctors, health officials, and pharmacists say that adverse side-effects are extremely rare. And most of the twentieth century parents accepted that pledge on

## Introduction

faith. For 100 years, almost everyone was pro-vaccination.

However, the internet has changed everything. Now parents can go online and chat with parents of vaccine-injured kids. They have discovered that adverse vaccine reactions are *not* extremely rare.

There are hundreds of thousands of vaccine-injured kids in the United States alone. This discovery led to the anti-vax movement organized by angry mothers who became warriors to protect their children. No one in their right mind will come between an angry mama bear and her cubs.

These women are knowledgeable and well-informed about vaccine side-effects especially regarding the mercury and aluminum ingredients in vaccines which are toxic to the human body. They have studied the science on ethyl mercury toxicity and understand the gulf of difference between the public presentation by the medical establishment and what the factual science says in 240 studies available on PubMed.

This book documents numerous scientific studies which clearly demonstrate that no remedy, including vaccination, is 100% safe and effective. That's why CDC health officials say that adverse side-effects are rare. But rare does mean exceptions – less than 100% safe. If vaccinations were 100% safe, effective, and risk free everyone would be pro-vaccine.

Numerous interviews with leading health officials, doctors, and parents who had negative vaccine experiences are also included herein. Now that we have established there's always some sort of risk, let's have a close look at the mandatory vaccine issue which is revoking a mother's right to avoid a potential risk to her child.

## Science Facts

Today there's a drive to mandate vaccines for every man, woman, and child.

However, the Association of American Physicians and Surgeons (AAPS) is not in favor of this premise, as stated in their *Fact Sheet on Mandatory Vaccinations*, April 9, 2009:

"AAPS has never taken an anti-vaccine position, although opponents have tried to paint that picture. AAPS has only attempted to halt government or school districts from blanket vaccine mandates that violate parental informed consent...

"The Centers for Disease Control admits that the reported number of adverse effects of vaccines is probably only 10% of actual adverse effects...

"Rampant conflicts of interest in the approval process have been the subject of several Congressional hearings, and a recent Congressional report concluded that the pharmaceutical industry has indeed exerted undue influence on mandatory vaccine legislation toward its own financial interests.

## Introduction

"The vaccine approval process has also been contaminated by flawed or incomplete clinical trials, and government officials have chosen to ignore negative results. For example, the CDC was forced to withdraw its recommendation of the rotavirus vaccine within one year of approval. Yet public documents obtained by AAPS show that the CDC was aware of alarmingly high intussusception rates months before the vaccine was approved and recommended.

"Mandatory vaccines violate the medical ethic of informed consent. A case could also be made that mandates for vaccines by school districts and legislatures is the de facto practice of medicine without a license."

Clearly, the AAPS does not favor mandatory vaccination, viewing it as violating medical ethics.

Similarly, a U.K. article by David Elliman and Helen Buford, discussed the fallout from mandatory vaccination. The article – *In Britain, Vaccinate with Persuasion, not Coercion* – published on March 23, 2014, is available at nytimes.com, and gives the following warning:

"Even where immunization is generally mandatory, in a free democracy, there has almost always been the provision for parents with conscientious objections to withhold their children from the immunization program.

"When smallpox vaccination was made compulsory in the 19th century in the United Kingdom, it was the poor who suffered. If they persisted in refusing immunization, they were fined or even sent to jail, for inability to pay.

"On the other hand, the affluent simply paid their fines and the children remained un-immunized. It was not long before conscience clauses were introduced and any element of compulsion abolished in 1948 with the introduction of the National Health Service.

"In an era when people are less accepting of authority and do not expect to do something because the government says so, trying to enforce immunization may actually make matters worse and create martyrs. Those who have genuine religious objections are unlikely to allow their children to be immunized, whatever the penalty.

"Parents who are hesitating about their vaccine decision because of concerns over vaccine safety may change their minds if given time and an opportunity to discuss their concerns with a well-informed health professional."

The comments are from leading authorities. David Elliman, MBBS, is a community pediatrician at Whittington Health in London and the immunization expert for the Royal College of Pediatrics and Child's Health. Helen Bedford, is a senior lecturer in children's health at University College, London Institute of Child Health.

Introduction

## Life is a Risk

Everything we do carries a risk, but in a democracy, we have choices. Why should vaccination be different from every other risk? When parents agree to vaccinate a child, it should not be due to intimidation, or by law. It must be their own free choice.

A child's life is more precious than anything else, so we must allow a choice whenever a potential risk is possible. Nobody wants their child to become ill. Everyone agrees with that.

Parents should be free to decide whether to vaccinate their kids. That's the reason this book is neither pro-vaccine nor anti-vaccine, but pro-vaccine-choice.

What if you're pressured against your own better judgement? Mandatory vaccination of children is an infringement of parental rights. It means denying parental guidance to choose what's best for our children.

To mandate vaccination, when families don't want it, is undemocratic and unwarranted. But more importantly, it's unethical because a child is not in the position to understand a decision made by strangers. A child only trusts the parents. If we undermine parental trust, we undermine the family unit; we undermine love and trust in society.

Mandatory vaccination is being presented as a public health issue but in reality, it's a human rights issue.

Pro-vaccine proponents say we shouldn't have a choice about vaccinating, even in a free society. They argue that wearing seatbelts to save lives is mandatory, and vaccines should be too.

This argument is known as the fallacy of false analogy. It's a common argument in which the analogy does not apply because it's poorly suited.

There are no adverse reactions from wearing a seatbelt. No injury can happen by wearing a seat belt when your car is in the garage. Injuries only happen because of driving accidents on the road that are the fault of drivers, not seatbelts.

Clearly, using compulsory seatbelts to argue for compulsory vaccines doesn't follow because they have nothing in common. It's the familiar false analogy argument that politicians and salespeople often use.

## Vaccine Safety

Everyone is pro public health, pro children's health, and pro immunity. So why do some people question the safety, efficacy, or even necessity of vaccination? Because they had a prior negative experience, or they know someone who had a negative experience, and they don't want to see it repeated.

To stamp caring individuals with a pejorative anti-vaxxer label when they only want healthy kids, is not only negative; it's extreme. Parents stamped with the anti-vax label were once pro-vaxxers. They changed

## Introduction

their stance when a child suffered an adverse reaction.

They found out the hard way by placing their children on the altar of vaccine propaganda. They sacrificed their child's future as well as their own future by blindly trusting doctors and health care providers.

Therefore, this book is pro-children's health as well as pro-vaccine-choice. Democracy is the exercise of freedom, and that makes mandatory vaccination a human rights issue.

Yet a huge backlash to the anti-vaccine movement is coming from health officials, pediatricians, and government agencies who promote vaccination for public health, and for profit. Too many pro-vax people are unsympathetic to parents whose kids had an adverse vaccine reaction.

Vaccination is a serious issue, but it's portrayed with petty, fundamentalist, black-and-white rhetoric. The issue is far more complicated than simple pro-vax or anti-vax labels. Knowledgeable persons don't frame the vaccine dialog in such polarizing terms because it's a complex subject.

Mary Holland, PhD, has examined the vaccination issue in detail. She's the Director of the Graduate Legal Skills Program at NYU and a Professor at the NYU School of Law. She earned her degrees at Harvard and Columbia Universities. Her research agenda has been vaccine law and policy, which resulted in her looking at the vaccine topic from various perspectives.

That's why Dr. Holland writes about the vaccine issue from the medical perspective, the scientific perspective, the ethical perspective, the religious perspective, the parent's perspective, children's perspective, philosophical perspective, legal perspective, and the business perspective because there's a lot going on with the topic today.

Can anyone be pro-vaccine over pro-children? I don't think that's rational. This is why parents need to understand the issues that confuse the vaccine debate. Our children need rational voices and empathetic hearts to represent them in a fight for which they have no say.

Why should you be interested in this? If you have ever felt unheard in your role as a parent, or frustrated, or uncomfortable, then you should understand the importance of parental instinct.

## Risks and Benefits

A mother's natural instinct is to protect and nurture her child, as well as to guard against what goes into baby's mouth. She wants to know if any substance will cause harm to her child.

Vaccination means unknown ingredients are going directly into the blood stream. Every parent should be extremely careful about vaccination because injecting directly into your baby's bloodstream is a far more

## Introduction

serious matter than what goes into baby's mouth. It's a cause for greater concern.

Do you know the ingredients in the vaccine shots your baby will get? The following image lists the ingredients in the MMR (measles, mumps, rubella) vaccine, published on the CDC Excipient Table at CDC.gov.

MMR (MMR-II)  chick embryo cell culture, WI-38 human diploid lung fibroblasts, vitamins, amino acids, fetal bovine serum, sucrose, glutamate, recombinant human albumin, neomycin, sorbitol, hydrolyzed gelatin, sodium phosphate, sodium chloride

Credit: CDC.gov

Besides DNA material from aborted chicken and cow embryos, there is human DNA as well. WI-38 comes from human abortions.

Some families may have no problem with these ingredients being injected into their babies, but others may object. That's why families need to be able to make an informed decision.

It's a good idea to understand the exact ingredients that labs use to make vaccines because the public has no idea of what's in vaccines. Chapter Seventeen contains every ingredient for each vaccine as supplied by the CDC website.

How does a parent evaluate vaccine side-effects compared to the promoted benefits? We want vaccines to be as safe as humanly possible for our kids, so do your research before those first shots.

Benefits never create a crisis. Risks create a crisis. Parents need to concentrate on vaccine risks before they make a risky choice. Doctors use benefits to influence parents. Benefits never harmed any child. Focus on the risks that harmed children of other families. Examine the side-effects on the printed vaccine insert, and discuss those risky side-effects with your doctor.

It's important to realize the consequences of these chemicals in a newborn's body. Deciding what will go into your little baby's delicate body is a very personal choice. Your decisions are critical as you guide your kids, so please make an informed choice to benefit them. Don't blindly accept that the shots injected into your baby are 100% safe.

People need to wake up about what's happening to babies around the world. Many problems in life are related to ignorance. This book is an inspired source of up-to-date knowledge for both parents and doctors who are really concerned about children's health.

Every child has a different body with a unique genetic makeup. As a parent, you know perfectly well that kids have varying degrees of tolerance for anything that enters their system. Nobody knows your child better than you do. Consequently, the one-size-fits-all

## Introduction

vaccination model can't possibly work the same for every youngster.

In an interview back in October 16, 2008, vaccine safety activist Barbara Loe Fisher explained that not all parents are in the same situation.

"Among us are parents with healthy children, and those with children who have been hurt by one-size-fits-all vaccine mandates that ignore the genetic and biological differences which make some people more vulnerable than others for having severe reactions to prescription drugs and vaccines."

Heartfelt interviews of parents with a vaccine-injured child will enlighten you about what occurred before and after the shots.

Although some people say vaccination is a controversial issue, there's no controversy about truth. They can doubt the truth, not like the truth, say it's not the truth, or that its controversial. Simply by labeling it as something else doesn't change the truth.

Most of the confusion around vaccine problems concern the following:

1) all relevant facts
2) differing opinions
3) risks and benefits of vaccinating
4) making a wrong decision

Therefore, a parent must do the research to make an informed decision before vaccinating their children. How to accomplish that?

This book explains foggy issues clearly and backs them up with authoritative scientific studies. The goal is to open your mind to hearing all sides. Knowledge empowers parents to make informed decisions based on the risks and benefits of any given medicine.

Equally important is recognizing your indispensable responsibility for the health of your children. It is not the function of corporations, politicians, or doctors to usurp that responsibility from parents. Who cares more for their kids than a parent?

Life is about choices. Democracy allows the fundamental freedom to choose your own lifestyle. When families agree to mandatory vaccination it redefines their children as property of the state. When the state can wield that kind of power over us, we have lost our basic right as custodian of our own body and our children's bodies.

"No American," Barbara Loe Fisher asserts, "should be legally forced to play vaccine roulette with a child's life...

"If we cannot be free to make informed, voluntary decisions about which pharmaceutical products we are willing to risk our lives for, then we are not free in any sense of the word. Because, if the State can tag, track down, and force individuals against their will to

## Introduction

be injected with biological products of unknown toxicity today, then there will be no limit on which individual freedoms the State can take away in the name of the greater good tomorrow."

If vaccines and vaccine policies are so wonderful there shouldn't be so many people asking so many questions. The truth is that many people know someone who was healthy, got vaxxed, and was never healthy again.

*Vaccines on Trial* offers a broad perspective to empower you to make an informed decision for your kids. You'll receive an excellent background to continue looking for answers for your particular situation. When you have a better understanding, your questions are met with better answers.

Essentially, the focus of this book is not about why parents object to vaccines. The focus is why leading doctors and researchers working in the field of immunization object to vaccines.

This book discusses controversial topics, which many state governments, doctors, and pharmaceutical companies do not discuss. They're afraid to speak about the adverse reactions to vaccination, as Dr. Bernadine Healy explains in Chapter Three.

The goal of *Vaccines on Trial* is to give every parent the most up-to-date information in as clear, concise, accurate, and unbiased manner as possible. You will hear from expert doctors and health officials who test vaccines scientifically.

If your choice is to vaccinate your kids, have your doctor check that your child is completely healthy before the shots. If there *is* an adverse reaction, your doctor can't say some precondition caused the reaction. You'll know for certain it was the vaccine. Immediately after the shot, ice the injection site to reduce the inflammation.

Now I'm not a doctor, a scientist, or an immunologist. However, as an investigative journalist, I do know how to research, how to dig behind the headlines, and how to present the facts to my readers in a clear, concise way.

Of course, no book can provide all the answers. But you'll find this to be an excellent introduction to the entire vaccine debate.

One last point. I funded all the research for this book myself, so you can be confident that I do not represent any corporate agenda.

What you read here is the unbiased truth, the whole truth, and nothing but the truth, like the required oath in every court of law.

# ~ 1 ~
# Herd Immunity

*It is difficult to get a man to understand something when his job depends on not understanding it.*

- Upton Sinclair

The difference between vaccination and medicine is that vaccines are given to healthy children and medicine is for sick children. Too many healthy children suffer severe side-effects, either physically or mentally. What I mean is that even one child suffering an adverse reaction is one too many.

Parents of children with adverse side-effects become strongly anti-vaccine, and with good reason. They had a direct experience that vaccines were not safe for their child. There are millions of such parents in America.

Then there are kids that have little or no side-effects from vaccines. Their parents give a resounding "Yes" to vaccinations and are pro-vaccine. Still, that doesn't guarantee vaccines are safe and effective for every child.

A third category consists of pro-vaccine advocates who use science, political lobbying, or fear of disease, to spread pro-vaccine propaganda. These people benefit financially from the vaccination business because they work within the pharmaceutical industry – it's their job. Make no mistake: producing, distributing, and administering vaccines is a multi-billion-dollar business.

One problem with many pro-vaccine advocates is their confrontational attitude. These pro-vax people deny or deride parents whose kids have experienced adverse vaccine side-effects. They will even attack the author of this book if they disagree with what they read, even though this book is only a written record of the existing documented experience of thousands. The attacks are always in the comments and reviews they post online.

Why do some people lack compassion for families who have had a beloved child undergo an adverse reaction after vaccination?

Why are some people so strongly against allowing individuals to make their own vaccination decision?

Let's look at two reasons why people are inflexible: fear of disease and financial gain.

First. If vaccines give immunity, then it's irrational for vaccinated people to fear contracting disease from others. The unvaccinated don't have this fear. People should feel protected and immunized if vaccine shots work as promoted. We pay for protection so why are we unsure those shots are protecting us?

To say that healthy unvaccinated children put the rest of us at risk means I lack faith in my own immunization. Some parents won't even let their child play with unvaccinated kids. They believe that an unvaccinated child who doesn't have a disease can give the disease they don't have to a child vaccinated for the disease. If the vaccine fails they blame the unvaccinated child who didn't have the disease. Such lack of faith borders on paranoia.

These people generally use pejorative language against the unvaccinated. They may speak the same against gays, blacks, Jews, or anybody with a different viewpoint.

Second. The need for financial gain weakens compassion for others. This translates into a lack of sympathy for parents of vaccine-injured kids. People may lash out at anyone who questions vaccines because this jeopardizes their job. We've all heard, "everyone has a price," and especially when the "price" includes their salary, or any financial benefit.

Why do people blame the unvaccinated for a resurgence of disease, when the unvaccinated child is perfectly healthy?

The answer is something else that's promoted by health officials as a public health issue. It's called herd immunity, or community immunity.

## Herd Immunity

According to the government website: vaccines.gov, herd immunity implies that when a critical portion of a community is immunized against a contagious disease, most members of the community are protected against the disease because there is little opportunity for an outbreak. Vaccination helps protect others in your community who are not vaccinated.

Herd immunity for protection of disease claims that chains of infection are likely to be disrupted, which stops or slows the spread of disease. In other words, the greater proportion of people vaccinated the smaller the probability that the unvaccinated will contract a disease. Is this a fact?

Let's hear what renowned Harvard immunologist Dr. Tetyana Obukhanych says in this regard.

"One of the most commonly used scare tactics employed by doctors is the alleged compromise of herd immunity. Parents are told that unvaccinated children 'parasitize' on the herd immunity established by vaccinated children, and endanger everyone else. Sadly, this issue then becomes an unwarranted source of strife between families with opposing views on vaccination.

"The truth is that for most communicable viral diseases, there is no herd immunity in post-elimination era. Herd immunity exists only when the proportion of individuals who are not susceptible to the virus is above 68%.

"Because live attenuated viral vaccines are given routinely only twice – at the age of one and five – and their protective effect against viral infections expires before adolescence, only vaccinated pre-adolescent children are resistant to viral infection.

"The adult population gradually becomes more and more susceptible, except those adults who had natural infection. Needless to say, pre-adolescents do not compromise 68% of the whole population, and cannot maintain herd immunity for the rest of the population. The apparent absence of major viral epidemics in the U.S. is now due to the absence of endemic viral exposure, not herd immunity."[1]

Dr. Russell Blaylock is a neurosurgeon and author. He agrees that herd immunity protection is not a fact and shows how the proof is right in front of our nose.

"That vaccine-induced herd immunity is mostly myth can be proven quite simply. When I was in medical school, we were taught that all of the childhood vaccines lasted a lifetime…It was not until relatively recently that it was discovered that most of these vaccines lost their effectiveness 2 to 10 years after being given.

"What this means is that at least half the population, that is the baby-boomers, have had no vaccine-induced immunity against any of these diseases for which they had been vaccinated very early in life. In essence, at least 50% or more of the population was unprotected for decades."[2]

The concept of herd immunity is based on the concept that contagiousness is the only way for disease to spread. There's no other way I can be exposed to the disease except by contracting it from someone who already has the disease.

Dr. Larry Palevsky argues that this claim "is the biggest problem regarding infectious diseases, contagiousness, and herd immunity. Because it doesn't allow for all the permutations, all the ways in which you could have a germ in your body and still *not* get sick."[3]

Exposure to disease also comes from the environment, not just proximity to a person who has the illness. Hence, the problem with herd immunity is the concept that the only vector of exposure is someone who already has the disease. People who have never studied immunology always have their own viewpoint on vaccine safety and effectiveness.

## Do Your Research

Health professionals promote vaccine safety because they have invested their life's work in sustaining the view that what they are doing is completely safe and for the greater good. Their credibility, career, and their income rests on public acceptance of vaccines.

Still, there are parents who say, *my doctor tells me vaccines are safe but I don't believe it.*

Then ask your doctor, *what's the basis for your confidence that vaccines are safe?* It might be what they taught back in medical school, or product publicity by a pharmaceutical company, or an article in a medical magazine.

Feel free to get into a conversation with your pediatrician because you are placing your baby's health in someone else's hands, instead of your own.

Doctors always say the vaccines they inject into your child's developing body is free from harmful side-effects. That's how they're trained. But when you chat online with parents whose child had a negative vaccine experience you can hear another side.

Your pediatrician has an obligation to review safety studies with you for any vaccine to be injected into your child. You have a right to know the actual science behind vaccine safety.

When doctors feel uneasy about your freedom to choose, we need to take a close look at why they're uncomfortable. It doesn't make sense for doctors to think an informed consent position is radical.

### Informed Consent

Everyone has to research a subject to come to an informed conclusion. Your child is worth all the effort you dedicate to this task.

Visit the CDC website to read the information on vaccines you're thinking to give your child. The CDC lists the ingredients for each vaccine on the excipient schedule: cdc.gov.

The ingredients information alone will open the minds of people whose eyes are closed. Besides chemicals like formaldehyde, mercury, and aluminum, there are also bovine extracts, a continuous line of monkey kidney cells, calf serum, and even human diploid fibroblast cell cultures (strain WI-38).

Many parents will be shocked to know that human aborted fetal tissue is used in some vaccines. This is of real concern for vegetarian, vegan, or religious parents. Naturally, they want to know which vaccines to avoid. See Chapter Seventeen to study the ingredient lists for every vaccine.

The National Vaccine Information Center (NVIC) website, nvic.org, is an excellent repository of relevant information where you can find out about vaccine ingredients.

Since 1982, the custodians of this website have been Informed Consent advocates and defend without compromise the legal right of every person to exercise freedom of choice when making a vaccination decision for themselves or their children even when contrary to federal recommendations.

NVIC provides counseling for parents reporting adverse vaccine side-effects, injuries, and death. To arrive at existential truth, you have to speak to people on all sides of the vaccine issue. So please get second and third opinions because only research can reveal hidden details.

Ultimately, to vax or not to vax is among the big decisions you'll make for your child. Certainly, not everyone has the time and energy to research thoroughly. Then, where do you put your faith and who do you trust?

The book you are now reading is a good start. I do not guarantee vaccines are 100% safe and effective, nor do I pretend that side-effects are extremely rare. You deserve to know what happens in those so-called rare cases of adverse side-effects. I've already done the research for you so this is a good starting point to begin your study.

In clinical trials, vaccines are tested one at a time. But on the CDC schedule, many vaccines are merged together, like MMR and DTaP (diphtheria, tetanus, pertussis). This combining effect has never been tested or studied for safety. And that is one cause for concern. There are others, too.

Newborns are receiving multi-dose shots of various vaccines all at once before they are even able to walk and talk. This vaccine layering affect has not been methodically tested in scientific studies. Thus, the long-term results are unknown and the risk of a serious adverse reaction increases.

Because the pharmaceutical industry has financed most of the vaccine research, this presents a tremendous bias dilemma.

My emphasis is on presenting scientific evidence to establish vaccine safety, efficacy, and more importantly, to understand the risks. However, it's vitally important to help your child build a strong natural immune system.

Viruses have been around mammals for millions of years; that's why nature developed the immune system for protection. The body has evolved to withstand and handle all the viruses and bacteria that come along.

Good health and wellness doesn't come from a hypodermic needle. It comes from vitamins, minerals, exercise, fresh air and sunshine. The body has an innate ability to heal. You cut yourself and the body heals that cut, automatically. As outside, so inside. The immune system works to heal the body internally. It's nature's way.

The immune system is predisposed to, and biased towards, health, rather than towards disease. So, let's keep our immune system strong.

If your family gives up junk food and switches to organic food as far as possible, your kids will develop stronger immune systems. It means you won't need to rely solely on vaccines for protection from disease. It's always better to be twice as safe.

Creating wellness and good health is the most powerful medicine at your disposal. The pills and shots model of medicine is not the wellness model. It's not "an ounce of prevention is worth a pound of cure" model of health.

Unfortunately, we live in a world where people don't use natural medicine and have no faith in their immune system or their body's ability to heal itself. They blindly believe vaccines are safe without doing the research. They blindly *believe* in science like people blindly believe in religion.

Science means there is an opportunity to objectively know reality through the scientific method. There are truths and falsehoods. Science allows us to distinguish between the two so the truth can be recognized. This scientific knowledge must be placed in the hands of the general public because we also believe in freedom.

Today the populace is increasingly misinformed scientifically. Moreover, the media, corporations, and governments take advantage of this to propagate dubious principles to promote coercive measures for their own benefit. That's the case with mandatory vaccination.

All persons are entitled to lead their life as they see fit because they are the only true possessor of their minds and bodies. Socio-economic control is as morally reprehensible as it is harmful in its social, economic, political, and environmental consequences.

Historically, science used to say that disease came from the gene factor. But genes don't cause epidemics. You need an environmental toxin in the body.

The latest data shows that disease is a result of epigenetic exposure – the environment acting upon our genes. In other words, 95% of our kid's problems come from epigenetic factors: fast food diet, video game lifestyle, and exposure to toxins.

This means that previous scientific beliefs have been replaced with updated paradigms. After a review of existing scientific data, the European Parliament has reversed its decision that pesticides benefit agriculture. Today's data shows that food grown with elevated pesticide levels adversely affects a child's developing brain.

Scientists in California have found that pregnant mothers who had traces of organo-phosphate metabolites (the basis for many pesticides) were more likely to have children with "adverse mental development at two years of age, attention problems at three-and-a-half and five years, and poorer intellectual development at seven years."

The new science always replaces the old outdated science. That's why we need to look at recent scientific studies to determine vaccine safety and efficacy. We can no longer blindly say, *I believe in science* and fail to do the research to fully understand the latest data.

Herd Immunity

# ~ 2 ~
# Undeniable Facts

*Whoever is careless with the truth in small matters cannot be trusted with important matters.*

*- Albert Einstein*

When you were a child did you have the chickenpox, or measles?

When I was a kid I only got the smallpox shots. I remember that because I was a small boy, not an infant. I never received vaccination for measles, chicken pox, whooping cough (pertussis), or the mumps. Neither did my sister, who was two years younger. Because those vaccines didn't exist when we were growing up. Nor did we get the polio shot.

I did get the measles and chicken pox, but so did most of the kids in my school. Other classmates got whooping cough or the mumps but I didn't. Neither my schoolmates nor I were impaired by these common childhood diseases.

How do I know? Because we all went to the same school from grades 1 through 12 together; as did my younger sister and her group of friends. Same thing for my cousins who lived in a different part of town. These are the early records of kids in the same age group from the same town before the advent of multiple vaccines.

I remember contracting poison ivy at summer camp. It wasn't fun, but it did leave me with lifetime immunity against the infection. That's how our body's immune system works.

Today, I'm a paragon of good health and so is my sister. In my entire life, I have never been to a hospital (except to visit others) and have never contracted a serious illness. If you received many shots as a child, are you a shining example of good health today?

You can ask friends and neighbors; *do you know people over 55 years of age*? Sure, and all of us had measles, chicken pox, mumps, etc. If these were so deadly before the MMR vaccine, would there be so many folks over 55 today? Because we had those diseases as kids, now all of us have lifelong immunity.

Back then families knew that once you got the measles or other childhood diseases, your immune system would fight off the "germs" and leave you with lifetime immunity. Doctors also knew it. When kids got the measles nobody thought, *Oh, my child might die*. Nobody considered such a thing. The treatment was lots of rest in bed, a healthy diet, and stay in your room so you won't affect others.

Of course, complications can arise from any disease which may lead to death in rare cases. But it's important to know that these childhood diseases are quite mild. Also, they confer the benefit of lifelong immunity so you never get the disease again.

Pro-vaccine advocates contend that the drop in the incidence of measles coincided with the licensing and wide use of a measles vaccine introduced in 1963. They fail to understand that mild childhood diseases like measles and pertussis strengthen a child's immune system and bestow natural immunity against the disease for life.

Vaccines cannot offer lifelong immunity. They require booster shots to boost the waning protection.

As an aside, many viral diseases are called childhood illnesses because prior to routine vaccination these diseases occurred mainly in children.

Dr. Tetyana Obukhanych explains that with the onset of routine vaccination, these benign childhood diseases have been pushed into adulthood where they can be more dangerous. She says that she contracted measles at the age of eleven despite being twice-vaccinated for measles at the age of two and five.

## Hidden Facts

Dr. Sherri Tenpenny, D.O., is a renowned researcher and author. Her research revealed that before the measles vaccine came out in 1963 the death for measles was three in ten million. She says the figure has not changed since then.

Some doctors quote a statistic that one in a thousand kids died from measles. People rewrite history and pull up statistics from refugees in the 1900s, or from backward countries with no sewage, no toilets, and no clean water. But these statistics do not represent developed countries with high standards of hygiene. Some statistics just magically appeared to support vaccine sales.

History means his story. Whoever is in power writes and presents his story (history). So much of history is absolutely from the perspective of the winner, the conqueror, or the promoter.

Dr. Tenpenny says, "I attribute my strong adult health to the fact that I had all the appropriate childhood diseases at the appropriate ages... That's how I developed such a strong and healthy immune system. The last time I had any illness at all was in 1977!"[4]

Yes, she's like the rest of us over 55. When the measles vaccine came on the market in the early 1960's sales were not good. People were not scared of childhood illnesses and nobody cared much about measles.

The American government started a deliberate scare campaign to convince everyone that measles was a dangerous disease. And ten years after, people lined up for the vaccine. Other countries quickly followed the American way. They always do.

Here's the thing: the vaccine wasn't invented because the disease was dangerous. The disease was made dangerous because there was a vaccine.

Similar story with chicken pox. The vaccine was initially offered as a convenience for working parents. But due to a lack of interest, all of a sudden chicken pox became a dangerous disease.

Yep, governments worldwide learned from the measles story and perfected the strategy to turn another benign disease into a danger to humanity.

*"You should get vaccinated against whooping cough (pertussis) to protect young babies!"* The current pertussis vaccine is acellular. Dr. Tetyana says it's designed to prevent disease symptoms, not to prevent infection.

Even if the vaccine did work (she says it doesn't) you still can't protect anyone else by getting this vaccine. The technical details of acellular pertussis are irrelevant because it's scientifically impossible. "It simply can't prevent infection, not even in theory," Dr. Tetyana clarifies.[5]

What does that mean? It means that pushing people to get the acellular pertussis vaccine (in DTaP) to protect their babies is quack medicine.

Our modern medical system is based on pharmaceuticals, which is described as evidence-based medicine. But really, it's patent-based medicine. Vaccine manufacturers are only interested in drugs and therapies that can be patented and can generate profits for the company. That's why the term profit-based medicine applies.

The pharmaceutical industry turns a blind eye to natural remedies. What they can't patent, they can't turn a profit. They have little interest in plant-based medicine because they can't patent plants to make money.

For companies, the overriding consideration is making a profit because that's what they're in business to do. Their line of work may be about public health but the shareholders want to see profits. That's why the worst thing that ever happened to public health was turning medicine and medical care into a business.

Currently, doctors advise families that vaccinating their children is the best thing they can do. Chapter Eight explains all the reasons doctors promote vaccination.

Parents are shocked when children experience adverse side-effects. The most devastating feeling is seeing your child in pain; being a witness to suffering that could have been avoided. Why should a parent feel guilty for doing what their doctor recommended?

## Undeniable Facts

Too many parents are filled with guilt for vaccinating their child, and wonder what to do next... after the fact.

They cry to their pediatrician, *this is what the vaccine did to my child*. A mother always knows when something bad happens to her child because she's with her baby 24 hours.

Pediatricians don't live with the kids that come into their office. Therefore, parents are horrified to hear their doctor's response which is usually one of the following: *the reaction is normal, it's temporary, it's not the vaccine, it's just a coincidence, it's a stage he's going through, the condition was already pre-existing in your child*, and more.

But who knows a child better than the mother? A doctor's trust and faith must reside in the mother's instinct. However, doctors are now usurping that instinct by asserting they know better. Their patronizing approach to medical care is inappropriate and wrong.

If your pediatrician says, *I know the science, I know the vaccines, I'm the doctor*, don't buy it. You know your child and the doctor doesn't.

You should trust your own instincts. Maternal instinct is the main reason humans have survived every calamity since time immemorial. Public health care has been in existence for less than 200 years. Mother's care has nurtured humanity since the very beginning.

Your questions and doubts are entirely valid because they come from parental instinct. So, let's look at some classified information about the CDC vaccine schedule to start our research.

## Vaccine Secrets

Did you know that the 1986 health Bill signed into law by President Ronald Reagan included a Vaccine Information Statement (VIS)? It's a concise statement of risks and benefits associated with each vaccine, including each dose in multi-dose vaccines like MMR and DPT, now DTaP.

By law, every parent should be shown the vaccine risks and benefits insert that comes with every vaccine before agreeing to vaccinate their kid. Why? So that pediatricians can administer vaccines with a parent's Informed Consent. What you don't understand, you can ask your doctor. It means you take your decision after understanding the information. Were you shown a vaccine risks and benefits sheet before your child got any shots?

Today, doctors simply assure families that vaccines are "safe and effective." You have to accept it on blind faith. Health providers claim that vaccinated children live healthier lives than unvaccinated kids. But in America there are *no* studies to scientifically compare which group is healthier. Please read the actual facts in Chapter Three.

## Undeniable Facts

How many parents, new mothers, or pregnant women know that the U.S. Supreme Court has legally classified all vaccines as "unavoidably unsafe?" Unavoidably means there is no way to avoid the fact that vaccines are unsafe. Yes, every vaccine administered by your pediatrician is legally classified as unsafe. Has your doctor told you?

It's your right to ask why your doctor claims the shots injected into your baby are safe when legally they are all "unavoidably unsafe." Chapter Seven reviews this Supreme Court ruling.

Has your doctor told you that you can no longer sue a vaccine company if their vaccine injures, or even kills, your child? Every vaccine manufacturer now has total immunity from any liability when something dreadful happens to your child.

Did you know that doctors also have complete immunity from lawsuits? You cannot sue doctors even if they coerce you to vaccinate your child against your better judgement. Do you think this is fair? The complete story is in this book.

How many readers know they have the right to file a petition to receive compensation for vaccine injuries? The 1986 Health Bill guarantees that children can receive damage benefits for vaccine injuries.

Has your pediatrician revealed that $3.56 billion has already been awarded to children injured by vaccines up to December 31, 2016? Although that's a huge amount of money, any harm to a child is unacceptable. And that money will not make a child normal again. Still, it's proof positive that vaccines carry a serious risk.

Despite the law, many injured kids are unable to receive compensation. Why not? Because it has become a bitter fight to get payment. Chapter Six reveals the facts you need to know.

Dr. Bernadine P. Healy has championed the principle that: "there may be susceptible children either genetically, metabolically, or due to mitochondrial disorders, immunological issues, or other issues that make them more susceptible to many vaccines, or to a particular vaccine, or even to an ingredient in vaccines, like mercury."[6]

Your child may be in the susceptible group of individuals that Dr. Healy affirms. How would you know? Sadly, no scientific studies or tests exist in the United States to settle this question. That's why you should be extra careful before vaccinating your kids.

So who is Dr. Healy? As a physician, cardiologist, and academic she became the first woman to lead the National Institutes of Health (NIH) and the first physician to lead the American Red Cross. She was a professor at Johns Hopkins University, Dean of the Ohio State University medical school, a White House science adviser, and also President of the American Heart Association.

In addition, she was the health editor and columnist for *U.S. News & World Report* and a well-known commentator in the media on health issues. Based on her qualifications, we should take her counsel seriously.

Dr. Healy was a member of the IOM (Institute of Medicine now renamed Academy of Medicine) when they issued a report in 2004 which basically said, "Do not pursue susceptibility groups. Don't look for those patients, those children who may be vulnerable."

However, she disagreed with that report. "I really take issue with that conclusion." In a TV interview she explained why she took issue.

"The reason why they didn't want to look for those susceptibility groups was because they were afraid that if they found them, however big or small they were, that would scare the public away."[7]

Since 2004, there have been a lot more disclosures to scare the public away. Has your health care counselor told you that scientists have now found retroviruses and neurotoxins in many of the common vaccines on the CDC schedule?

Vaccines can be contaminated with bacterial and viral fragments. Even human and animal DNA have been detected, so we know that vaccines are not always sterile. Chapter Fourteen explains the toxic ingredients issues with which you should be familiar.

Dr. Paul Thomas is a board-certified pediatrician for over 30 years. He has authored several books, is the founder of Physicians for Informed Consent, and a member of the Academy of Pediatrics. His ambition is for parents and physicians to be better informed before vaccinating youngsters.

He points out that it's the duty of the Academy of Pediatrics to be the organization that guards the health of children. That's why he gives parents a vaccine information statement to study before he administers any shots to their child.

"Unfortunately," he exclaims, "most of my peers don't even realize there's aluminum in these vaccines. Or if they do, they don't know how much is in there..." He's talking about his peers at the Academy of Pediatrics, folks.

When he was in medical school they taught that it was safe to inject infants with vaccines containing aluminum. Today it's classified as a neurotoxin.

"They don't know what the safe dose is for aluminum," Thomas explains, "because, you see, we were trained that aluminum is safe! It's been in vaccines since the beginning, and it was studied and was proven to be safe. At least that's what we were told."[8]

Most doctors simply accept what they are told but Dr. Thomas decided to do his own research. "I have two books, entire books, just on aluminum toxicity." He discovered what they taught in med school was not a fact.

The journal, *Current Medical Chemistry*, published a study that children up to 6 months of age receive 14.7 to 49 times more aluminum from vaccines than is allowed by FDA (Food and Drug Administration) safety regulations.

By adding aluminum to a vaccine, it acts as an adjuvant for the immune system. Adjuvants are ingredients that are added to vaccines to facilitate a strong immune response in the body. The CDC says that adjuvants help vaccines work better and that's why they've been used for decades.

Europeans have lots of data on the use of adjuvants especially among the elderly, but immunologist Anthony S. Fauci is dubious about their use with children. "I don't think anybody has really good data on adjuvants in children."

In any circumstance, the immune response to an adjuvant is hard on the body and always causes inflammation. Hence, vaccines are inflammatory. They are meant to be in order to cause a response in the body. That's how they work. This introduces a potential risk concerning the delicate body of a developing infant.

On the other hand, science knows that aluminum is toxic to the human body. The problem we face for children is that aluminum as an adjuvant is not only toxic but it accumulates in their tiny body.

So while your pediatricians and health care agencies insist that aluminum in vaccines is "safe," we get a far different story from independent scientific research studies published in *Current Medical Chemistry*.

Why is there a discrepancy between scientific studies and local health officials? Because something else is in play behind the scenes – vaccination as a business.

If your vaccinated child suffered an adverse reaction, and now has a chronic health condition, it could be the result of the aluminum adjuvant.

Dr. Thomas revealed that med schools teach that aluminum in vaccines is safe. This raises the question, what are med students actually taught about vaccines?

If you want to see what courses students study in medical school, you can simply search the current curriculum of any university online. Let's look at one of the best in the country, Harvard Medical School.

First year students study the following thirteen courses:

- Introduction to The Profession
- The Molecular and Cellular Basis of Medicine
- The Human Body
- Human Genetics
- Patient-Doctor 1

- Introduction to Social Medicine and Global Health
- Clinical Epidemiology and Population Health
- Introduction to Healthcare Policy
- Scholarship in Medicine
- Physician and Community
- Integrated Human Physiology
- Immunology, Microbiology, and Pathology
- Medical Ethics and Professionalism

In Harvard's five-year curriculum whatever med students are taught about vaccines and vaccination is contained in one first year course: Immunology, Microbiology, and Pathology.

You can search the curriculum of any university you choose and you'll see there's not much variation from Harvard. The topic of vaccines and vaccination is not prominently featured in the education of potential doctors. They have studied very little about the topic. That's the reason they just say what they've been taught – that it's safe and effective.

## Preventative Medicine

If you have a healthy child and want to prevent an adverse reaction that could develop into a chronic health condition in the future, the best medicine is prevention. It's your choice – you can pay for an ounce of prevention or a pound of cure.

To decrease and stop the cumulative effects of toxins in your child's body, you may want to consider a detox. Accumulated toxins contribute to adverse health conditions. That's why we need to address the vaccination burden on your kids from the toxins stored in their body from the shots.

In natural medicine, disease has one of two underlying causes: toxicity and nutritional deficiency. Vaccination is, in a word, toxic. Detoxing can restore equilibrium by supporting the body's elimination channels. Toxins can then safely be removed from the body.

With children, it's extremely important to detox in a slow, long-term, and gentle manner. Establishing care with a Naturopath, a Naturopathic Physician, or a Chiropractor trained in detoxing is the safest and best idea.

Even if aluminum helps vaccines work better, I don't want it in my baby's tender body because it's a known neurotoxin. Aluminum is a heavy metal that's never had a function in the human body since the beginning of time. It can only throw a baby's developing immune system into disarray.

Dr. Thomas is quite upset that aluminum is still added to vaccines. Does it bother you?

In France, there's a moratorium on all vaccines with aluminum. Their studies show that aluminum leads to complications that can cause neurotoxicity, autism, and even death. Back in the U.S.A., however, vaccines still contain aluminum. Why do French kids have protection superior to that of American kids? Chapter Eleven reveals the whole story.

All good science and common sense warns us that injecting chemicals into newborns, as well as pregnant women with a growing fetus, is a huge red flag. It can be catastrophic to that delicate new life.

You might want to ask your pediatrician if he knows:

1) that aluminum is a neurotoxin
2) whether it's included in the vaccines he administers to children

Remember, your doctor doesn't care for your child more than you.

### Autism Secrets

The 1988 movie "Rain Man," starring Dustin Hoffman and Tom Cruise, introduced the term autism to the public. People heard the word autistic and strived to understand what it meant.

In the 1980s the autism rate in the U.S. was 1 in 10,000 children. It was a relatively rare disorder. In 2012, 1 in 68 children became autistic according to the CDC website.[9] That's a dramatic upturn since the 1980s. For 2018, some scientists say it will be 1 in 25. Clearly, we are in the midst of an autism epidemic.

Medical science says there's no link between autism and childhood vaccines. They also state that the cause of autism is unknown. We are left with this quandary

– the CDC doesn't know what causes autism yet they assure us that it's not vaccines.

The correlation that autism has increased as the number of vaccines has increased, is not accepted as causative by pro-vaccine advocates. Doctors, scientist, and parents are now engaged in a raging debate whether childhood vaccines are causing autism. Of course, if science can't pinpoint the cause of autism, then we have cause for doubt.

That leaves us with no other choice but to accept the correlation with vaccines containing thimerosal as a starting point for autism. The fastest way to scientifically prove that thimerosal is not the cause is to remove it from vaccines and see if autism symptoms greatly diminish. Within 6 short months we will have found our answer scientifically.

Parents plead with health officials, *if mercury is in doubt then please take it out*. But their voices fall on deaf ears. Why this insistence to keep thimerosal in vaccines?

Parents also protest that children are too young to get so many vaccines. Their battle cry is, *too many vaccines given too soon*. But that also falls on deaf ears. Why can't the CDC spread out the vaccines over a longer period of time? There must be a hidden agenda to continue without change because at face value the present policy has zero logic.

## Undeniable Facts

Dr. Paul Offit, M.D., is Chief of the Division of Infectious Diseases at the Children's Hospital of Philadelphia. In his opinion, "Vaccines, I would argue, are the safest, best-tested things we would put into our body. Obviously, nothing is absolutely safe."

Well, if nothing is absolutely safe, then why not take thimerosal out to scientifically judge the difference?

Vaccines are used in the fight against infectious diseases. Many people fear that without them we could see the return of disease like polio and smallpox. However, it may well be that it's not the vaccine that's harmful to children, rather it's the mercury based ingredient thimerosal that's the source of all the suffering.

In an interview for the documentary "Trace Amounts," Offit opines that small quantities of toxins don't pose a genuine threat. He claims the amount of mercury in thimerosal is so small that it's really no cause for concern. It's when toxins appear in larger quantities that they become dangerous.

He gives the following example: "If I drank two gallons of water without replacing the sodium and other specific minerals that are there, so if I lower all my mineral contents so I get a seizure, does that mean water is a neurotoxin? No."

Of course, the remedy to his argument would be to stop drinking two gallons of water to prevent having a seizure. Similarly, let's stop injecting children with thimerosal laced vaccines, as a scientific experiment, and see whether that results in a reduction of autistic symptoms. If you don't do the test, you can't say what's best.

Clearly, Offit is not concerned about thimerosal in childhood vaccines. Yet, he's the Chief medical official at Children's Hospital in Philadelphia. Would you trust him with the health of your child?

Although we now know that smoking can cause lung cancer, not everyone who smokes suffers from lung cancer. Similarly, not everyone who gets a vaccine suffers from autism. The answer is susceptibility! This is exactly what Dr. Bernadine Healy proposed back in 2009.

The CDC now says that no further studies need to be done because we know that thimerosal is not the cause of autism. In science you never say, *no further studies should ever be done*. By calling a halt to the studies you know they're trying to hide a problem.

The CDC website has a specific page on thimerosal and thimerosal exposure. They report that there is no harm caused by thimerosal, except for occasional redness and swelling at the injection site.

But look at the insert that comes with the vaccine before you accept a shot. Analyze the side-effects. When one of the side-effects is death, don't take that risk. The reason death is listed as a side-effect is because some kids have died. If you're children are healthy now, why take unnecessary risks? Remember, it only takes one shot to trigger an unwelcome side-effect.

How did this autism epidemic explode in the last three decades, and what is the cause? Scientists admit they do not know what causes autism, but they do admit it has become an epidemic of epic proportions.

Autism is a devastating disorder that destroys families. Yet it could be completely prevented. The most compelling factor in the fight against autism is that we can pinpoint the cause to the mother's story that her child developed autistic symptoms after a vaccination.

We don't notice autistic symptoms before vaccination. So, once we recognize inoculation as a contributing cause, then we can remove that influence to prevent the ongoing autism epidemic. Of course, we may not know which vaccines are the direct cause. But we can surely begin to remove all traces of neurotoxins like mercury and aluminum from every vaccine as an earnest start.

Specifically, ethyl mercury in thimerosal and polysorbate 80 need to be banned from vaccines. No study has ever been done to validate that thimerosal is harmless.

Studies do show that both mercury and polysorbate 80 breach the blood brain barrier to affect 1) the way a child's brain develops, and 2) how the immune system develops. We know this for a fact from studies because polysorbate 80 is used in chemotherapy for the specific reason that it breaches the blood brain barrier.

When we inject our kids with a cocktail of live viral vaccines, like MMR or DTaP, and chemicals like mercury or aluminum, the immune system can go into shock. It may not cope because in the entire history of humanity such chemicals were never launched into a living body. And now they're injected at the same time as a multi-dose?

## Unvaccinated Children

Our children are the most cherished gift we will ever receive. They are the future of our country. Do you think it's wise to minimize a child's immune system? Our kids rely upon us to make the right choices for their health.

Dr. Heather Wolfson is a holistic family care expert. She grew up in a family that believed in fostering good health with a strong immune system. Her parents did not receive any vaccinations and they didn't give young Heather, or her brothers and sister, any shots when they were growing up. Everyone in the entire family is strong and healthy.

Today she is a practicing doctor in Arizona with a family practice where she teaches families about health and wellness. Her husband is Dr. Jack Wolfson, a board-certified cardiologist, who gave up recommending drugs and vaccines when he saw the positive results of good health and a strong immune system.

For the last twelve years these two doctors have been giving seminars about the positive benefits of *not* vaccinating.

**Dr. H. Wolfson:** "I've had many people come up to me and say; *this is my son who's now ten and I didn't vaccinate him because I attended your seminar*. We've been doing this seminar for almost twelve years now. Our latest seminar last month was sold out – 250 tickets. With each one we do, I hope it only gets larger and larger. And it's very rewarding. It is beautiful to see those unvaccinated children with that bright look in their eyes, and for the parents to tell me all the stories of how healthy their kids are, and the difference between their children and the vaccinated population. It's beautiful."

What more proof do we need? As a parent, you know that everywhere you look – in magazines, on TV, in news reports, online, – everybody insists it's best to vaccinate your kids. You might be thinking; *how can I understand that it's better not to vaccinate?*

Well, to arrive at a correct decision about anything, you must hear all sides of the story. That's what they do in a court of law.

Have you spoken to or heard from a parent whose children had adverse vaccine side-effects?

In a debate both sides present their facts and opinions, so people can take a decision after understanding the claims from all sides. If we only hear from one side, and ignore the other side, then we won't be able to fully grasp the big picture.

In this book you will hear from leading scientists in their field, as well as professionals working in public service, who all had a child that was vaccine damaged.

Dr. Brian Hooker has a PhD in biochemical engineering. He has conducted biotechnology research for over 25 years in environmental restoration and plant genetic engineering as a senior research scientist at Pacific Northwest National Laboratory. Today he is an Associate Professor of Biology at Simpson University.

Gayle Delong, PhD, is an Associate Professor at Baruch College who has authored several impressive statistical studies. She won an award for her paper, *The Conflict of Interest Financially in the Vaccine Industry*. Another paper, *The Statistical Analysis Making an Association Between Vaccines and Autism*, confirmed the contributing factor of vaccines on autism.

Barbara Loe Fisher is a founding member and President of the NVIC. She worked with Congress on the 1986 Health Act to include legislation that compensated children with injuries after vaccination.

These are not crackpot people but leading authorities in their profession whose children were damaged by vaccines. That's when they took up the fight to protect other children, your children, from vaccine injury. Their stories illustrate that vaccines are not as safe as promoted.

## Media Secrets

A question that always comes up is, why do public health officials claim that vaccines are safe and effective? Surely, they understand the entire issue.

Nobody shows TV interviews with parents of children injured by vaccination. We never see or hear any terrible news of kids injured after a shot. Why not? Well, who is the media's #1 advertiser?

For media outlets, 70-80% of their advertising revenue comes from pharmaceutical brands. You've seen the ads for drugs and meds on TV and in magazines. That's why every news outlet has its hands tied. They can't risk losing their advertising dollars so they don't cover the vaccine injury story.

With the exception of CBS, every major media outlet has at least one board member who is a drug company insider. It's a major conflict of interest and should never be allowed, but it's common practice in corporate America.

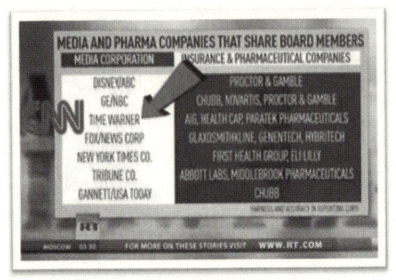

Credit. www.rt.com

Your local news anchors are trained not to say anything negative about the sponsors, or about the sponsor's products. If they don't follow protocol, they risk losing their job.

That's why they always show something positive about the sponsor's product like smiling kids happily receiving their medicine. Does that sound like your child?

Moreover, students studying in med school, and interns in hospitals, never even discuss vaccinations. It's accepted as medical dogma; they are safe, effective, and appropriate. There's no talk about risk, or about ingredients in the vaccines. What's the reason?

## Undeniable Facts

Perhaps, you are unaware that universities and medical schools nationwide receive grants and financial disbursements from the pharmaceutical industry. Naturally, schools don't bite the hand that feeds them.

It's a well-known fact that many doctors don't read their own medical journals. Of course, they are voluminous and dry so busy doctors just don't have the time to sit and read.

That's why many are not up-to-date with the latest scientific advances in their own medical literature. They simply believe what they were told in medical school, which may be a decade or two back, sometimes more.

When doctors have their own kids, however, it's different. That's much closer to home. Now, they begin researching to get all the facts. So, here's the last secret in this chapter. Many doctors don't vaccinate their own kids according to the CDC schedule that they recommend for your kid. The whole story is in Chapter Nine.

Many doctors will push a parent to vaccinate their kid by using fear; *if you don't vaccinate, your child could suffer a terrible disease.* But when you do the research, you discover that leading doctors are also vaccine hesitant.

There's no reason to fear because your immune system has the natural ability to fight disease better than injecting chemical substances into the body.

Toxins can cause autoimmune diseases, sterility, seizures and even death. Those are the listed side-effects on printed vaccine inserts. Why are they listed? Because that's what happened in some cases.

Autoimmune disease is defined as the immune response of an organism against any of its own tissues, cells, or cell components. Autoimmune diseases like rheumatoid arthritis, diabetes, and inflammatory bowel disease are on the rise. Our immune system is fighting the meds we inject.

A recent scientific paradigm known as the Hygiene Hypothesis claims that in countries where kids get measles, mumps, rubella, and chickenpox as toddlers, they have far less autoimmunity as adults. The premise is that benign childhood diseases influence our immune cells to regulate a healthy immune response that later in life reduces autoimmunity.

It's an important hypothesis because society may be conducting an unintentional experiment. By removing infections with antibiotics and vaccines we may be altering the maturation process of our immune cells, thereby increasing the risk of autoimmunity. That's in addition to the nutrient deficiencies coming from a modern diet of fast food, sugary soda drinks, and a toxin laden environment.

So on one hand, vaccines may confer public health benefits. On the other hand, there are risks that haven't been adequately qualified in relation to the hygiene hypothesis, the adjuvant question, and shots for benign children's diseases which are not fatal.

## Side-Effect Secrets

You probably know about SIDS. When we look at vaccine side-effects, one of them is death. Because that's what happened in some cases. But don't take my word for it, look at the vaccine insert that comes in every packet and read the listed side-effects and ingredients. You can ask your doctor to explain it all.

If you are a pregnant woman, a mother who has recently given birth, a parent who has youngsters, a grandparent expecting grandkids, a nurse working in a maternity ward or in a children's hospital, a pediatrician who administers all manner of vaccines, or a doctor who should be well-informed about public health concerns, then you owe it to the children to be fully up-to-date about the latest vaccine research and to question why so many shots are necessary.

After you understand what's in the vaccine you're about to give your child, and what the side-effects are, then make your own informed decision. That's democracy in action.

Remember, it just takes one vaccine to harm a youngster. So, before you give your lovely child all 69 shots be absolutely certain that the benefits outweigh the risks. If something undesirable happens to your kid, you will live with that for the rest of your life. So please be fully informed.

Side-effects are printed for two important reasons:
- because they happened before to other children
- as a warning, to free the vaccine company from blame

Now you know a few more reasons why you should study the vaccine issue. It's always best to make an informed decision after understanding the risks.

Although I'm not a doctor, everything in this book comes from leading health officials and medical professionals renowned in their field, like Dr. Healy, Dr. Thomas, and many others. Obviously, one doesn't have to be a doctor to know when a child is sick, or is suffering. Every parent knows that.

Therefore, this book champions a parent's right to selectively choose to accept the full vaccine schedule, to delay some vaccines, or to skip vaccines, based on their research and belief system. After all, America is not a fascist country. We believe in democracy.

Two paths illuminate the correct conclusion on who benefits most from vaccination: 1) follow the health, and 2) follow the money. In this book, we do both.

## ~ 3 ~
## Vaccine Verification

*The only safe vaccine is a vaccine that is never used.*

- James R. Shannon
National Institutes of Health (NIH)

I'm sure you want the best health for your kids. Who is healthier, a vaccinated child or an unvaccinated child? This is the first issue we will examine. A scientific study should determine the reality.

According to Dr. Chad F. Rohlfsen, in Des Moines, Iowa, there is a difference between a mother who is looking after the long-term health interest of her child versus parents who neglect to do that and rely on their local Department of Health and Human Services for health information.

The HHS only tells you half the story. For instance, they project that vaccinated children are healthier. Maybe your doctor also mentioned that. Of course, the idea that humans can inject themselves to better health is an extreme belief.

It's remarkable, however, that no major study in America has compared vaccinated and unvaccinated children to see who retained better health years later. So, there *is no proof* vaccinated children are healthier.

Dr. Rohlfsen tells us that Iowa has 3,400 unvaccinated children on record within the school system. Epidemiologists can easily conduct a study to determine whether vaccinated kids are healthier than unvaccinated kids. However, there's no major study available in any state. Why not?

Bestselling author and Health Educator David Wolfe questions, "Why can't we do rigorous scientific studies with one group that's vaccinated and one group that's not?" Because that's what science does.

Wolfe desires to see comparative studies on every vaccine administered today. For some mysterious reason, nobody does these studies and he wants to know why. Who is afraid of the results? Is there something to hide?

Obviously, if vaccinated children live healthier and longer lives that data would be invaluable for vaccine manufacturers. It would prove their product is superior for health: *now get with the program and vaccinate your kids.* So why don't they do the studies? It seems so logical, both business-wise and health-wise.

Yet there are no scientific studies comparing unvaccinated children with children on the vaccine schedule. Does that sound irresponsible? Of course, if unvaccinated kids were healthier that would be bad for business and for the shareholders.

Pharmaceutical companies are in business to sell their vaccines, drugs, and remedies. The profits pay salaries which pay mortgages, car payments, their kid's college education, clothing, food, vacations, and of course, luxuries. In other words, everything needed to support a lifestyle and a family.

## Update

Suddenly, on April 27/2017, the *Journal of Translational Science* published the first comparative study of vaccinated and unvaccinated kids in America. Sadly, this report is not well-publicized but we'll look at the results here.[10]

Dr. Andrew R. Mawson and his team of epidemiologists from the School of Public Health at Jackson State University compared 666 unvaccinated and vaccinated homeschooled children from Oregon, Florida, Louisiana, and Mississippi.

Dr. Mawson is a distinguished epidemiologist with an extensive record in children's health research. His study assessed the overall health of three groups: unvaccinated kids, fully vaccinated kids, and partially vaccinated kids, from the age of 6 to 12. Each group comprised one third of the sample population.

In order to find a large population of children who hadn't received any vaccines, the Jackson State scientists utilized Homeschool organizations in four states and compared the incidence on a broad range of health outcomes for all the children.

The conclusion of the research was that vaccinated children were *more* inclined to be diagnosed with a chronic illness than unvaccinated children. The published results showed that vaccinated children were:

- 4.2-fold more likely to be diagnosed on the Autism Spectrum
- 340 percent more likely to be diagnosed with ADHD
- 5-fold more likely to be diagnosed with a learning disability

The study also disclosed that vaccinated kids had increased risk for common disorders:

- 2.4-fold more likely to be diagnosed with any chronic illness
- 2.9-fold more likely to be diagnosed with Eczema
- 3.7-fold more likely to acquire Neuro-developmental Disorder
- 3.8-fold more likely to be diagnosed with middle ear infection
- 5.9-fold more likely to have been diagnosed with pneumonia
- 700 percent more likely for surgery to insert ear drainage tubes

- 22-fold more likely to require an allergy medication
- 30-fold more likely to be diagnosed with allergic rhinitis (hay fever)

Surprisingly, the unvaccinated group was medically superior in every category measured. This is exactly what Dr. Heather Wolfson was talking about in Chapter One.

You can view the results of this study at: http://info.cmsri.org/vaccinated-vs.-unvaccinated

The study suggests that fully vaccinated children may be trading in the prevention of benign childhood illnesses like measles, chicken pox, and pertussis for chronic disorders like ADHD and Autism.

The Jackson State scientists called for more scientific studies to help explain and clarify these findings.

## Studies Around the World

In other countries, studies have also shown that unvaccinated kids are healthier than their vaccinated friends.

As far back as 1992, the Immunization Awareness Society (IAS) of New Zealand conducted a survey to examine children's health. The study indicated that vaccinated children were more likely to suffer from asthma, eczema, ear infections, hyperactivity and other chronic conditions.

The study showed a ten-fold increase in tonsillitis infections among vaccinated children and a complete lack of tonsillectomy operations with unvaccinated children.

Researchers discovered that 92% of children needing a tonsillectomy operation had been vaccinated for measles, indicating that the measles vaccine may have made some children more susceptible to tonsillitis.

A total of 245 families returned questionnaires on various health questions, giving the researchers a total of 495 children surveyed. Of these, 226 were vaccinated and 269 were unvaccinated, 273 were males and 216 were females. (Six children were not classified)

Journalist Sue Claridge reported on the study:

"Respondents were asked to provide the year of birth, gender, vaccinations received, whether or not the child suffered from a range of chronic conditions (asthma, eczema, ear infections/glue ear, recurring tonsillitis, hyperactivity, diabetes or epilepsy) whether or not he or she needed grommets, had had a tonsillectomy, or were shown to develop motor skills (walking, crawling, sitting-up etc.). Parents also provided information on breastfeeding and bottle feeding and when a child was weaned if breastfed."

The study revealed that 81 families had both vaccinated and unvaccinated kids. Many families vaccinated an older child yet were reluctant to vaccinate their younger child due to growing concerns about vaccine safety.

Researchers concluded that: "While this was a very limited study, particularly in terms of the numbers of unvaccinated children that were involved and the range of chronic conditions investigated, it provides solid scientific evidence in support of considerable anecdotal evidence that unvaccinated children are healthier that their vaccinated peers."[11]

In September 2011, German researchers did a longitudinal study of 8000 unvaccinated children from birth to age 19. Researchers conducted a survey using questionnaires to gather their data s in the New Zealand study. Once again, results showed vaccinated children to be up to five times more likely to suffer from diseases and disorders than their unvaccinated peers.[12]

American critics dismiss such survey studies as being purely epidemiological. Leading government agencies (CDC and FDA) repeatedly state that studies comparing vaccinated children to unvaccinated children shouldn't take place for ethical reasons.

Even so, whenever researchers take it upon themselves to do these studies the unvaccinated children always fare better than the vaccinated.[13]

Most people don't know that research studies confirm unvaccinated kids are much healthier. Why? Because pharmaceutical companies choose to keep it quiet.

Regardless of what health officials may say, a parent should always have the final decision for their children.

## Measles Cases

Let's look at the 2014 measles outbreaks in the U.S. There were 644 cases of measles in 27 states that year. The largest outbreaks were at an Amish community in Ohio and at Disneyland in California.

So, 383 people fell ill after unvaccinated Amish persons returned from the Philippines with the illness. The outbreak received far less attention than the Disneyland episode because it posed far less threat beyond the isolated Amish community. No deaths were reported.

NBC News broadcast that the Disneyland outbreak had "sickened 147 people in the U.S. There were no deaths." We rarely find that measles will lead to death. The CDC website provides the following information for the Disneyland outbreak:

"Among the 110 California patients, 49 (45%) were unvaccinated." The CDC noted that of the unvaccinated 37 were vaccine-eligible and 28 were intentionally unvaccinated because of personal beliefs. One was on an alternative vaccination plan.

These figures show that 55% of the patients *were* vaccinated, yet they still got infected by measles. Ironically, more vaccinated patients had the disease than the unvaccinated. It wasn't a failure to vaccinate; it was a failure of the vaccine.

Commenting on the Disneyland outbreak, Dr. Gregory Wallace of the CDC said it was bad luck for those that caught the disease. "But you make your own bad luck, too," he quipped, inferring that it's bad luck to not be vaccinated for measles.

It's quite clear, however, that the vaccine didn't protect the vaccinated group. This is a common occurrence as you'll soon discover.

Perhaps you noted that those who paid good money to get vaccinated still got the disease. There were no deaths, and whoever did get the measles were now immunized for life. So, the infinitesimal risk of injury from measles compared to the huge benefit of getting lifelong immunity makes it an easy decision for a parent.

Author Neil Z. Miller is the Director of the Think Twice Global Vaccine Institute. His book, *Critical Vaccine Studies*, reviews thousands of people who contracted measles or chicken pox as kids. This group was compared to persons who didn't get these childhood diseases.

The book has 400 case studies showing that vaccinated people end up with more health problems later in life.

Miller says he compiled these studies because he got tired of hearing doctors say there's no studies proving vaccines are unsafe. He unequivocally declares that over a thousand studies published in peer-review journals document problems with vaccine safety and efficacy.

Credit: http://amazon.com

He points out that when kids get measles or chicken pox the disease stimulates the immune system to protect them for the rest of their life. They are even less likely to develop different cancers. Miller has several documented studies which prove that such people are also protected against cardiovascular disease.

The CDC does admit that anyone born before 1957 has "presumptive evidence of immunity" against measles. Like me, my sister, Dr. Tenpenny, and everyone else from our generation before the measles vaccine existed.

Unfortunately, when children are vaccinated against the common childhood diseases the vaccines do not stimulate the immune system to give lifetime protection. That's why the youngsters have to get booster shots to maintain some form of protection, although not lifelong.

## Infant Mortality

In 2011, Miller co-authored another book with Dr. Gary Goldman. They looked at the vaccination schedules of different nations to see how many vaccines they gave to infants. A baby that's less than one year of age is considered an infant.

They compared infant mortality rates for first world nations with the number of vaccine doses given. Infant mortality is measured by the number of deaths per one thousand live births.

At the time of the study several European nations required only 12 shots for their infants. In contrast, U.S. medical authorities gave 26 shots to protect infants from infectious diseases that could cause death.

The researchers originally assumed that the U.S. had the best infant mortality rate. Therefore, they wanted to study the difference between countries that require 12 infant shots versus a nation that requires 26 shots.

To their surprise, Miller and Goldberg discovered that 33 nations had a better infant mortality rate than the United States. Although the U.S. requires the most vaccines for their infants they ranked 34th for infant mortality among first world nations. Discovering that the U.S. had a worse record than 33 other countries was a shock to the researchers.

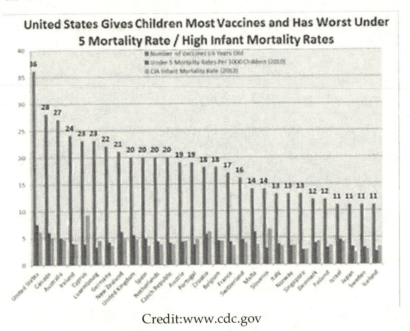

Credit:www.cdc.gov

Countries like Israel, Japan, Sweden, and Iceland (far right of graph) had much better infant mortality rates with only 11 vaccines for childhood diseases than the U.S. using 36 vaccines (far left of graph).

The study revealed a significant correlation between the number of vaccine doses a nation requires and that nation's infant mortality rate. The least number of shots given by first world nations correlated with the best infant mortality rate. Nations demanding more shots had worse infant mortality rates.

These studies were published in peer-reviewed journals so that doctors and health authorities could analyze the studies. Despite these results the CDC vaccine schedule continues to give American babies more vaccines than other first world countries.

## CDC Vaccine Schedule

In the 1950s American children were fully vaccinated with only 2 or 3 shots. By 1986 that number had increased to 10 shots.

Today the federal government says that all children by the age of 18 should have 69 doses of 16 different vaccines. And 49 of those doses are given before age 6. It's a pharmaceutical company's dream come true. Sales are going through the roof and even more vaccines are coming which we detail in Chapter Twelve.

Statistics also show that over 8.3 million American teen-agers under 18 are on a psychiatric drug of some kind. One in four kids takes at least one prescription drug in any given month.

Our grandparents never took these drugs, because they didn't exist back then, yet they are alive and well to question why youngsters need these drugs today.

Did you know that the FDA doesn't classify vaccines as drugs? Many health authorities want to reclassify vaccines as drugs because drugs go through stringent testing before coming on the market. Vaccines require very little testing before they are offered for sale.

Over the years we have seen a dramatic increase of children's vaccines on the CDC schedule. At the same time, undesirable side-effects are progressively escalating. Is this increase warranted?

As President of the NVIC, Barbara Loe Fisher puts the number of vaccine shots in perspective. "When my children were receiving vaccines in the late 70s and 80s, it was 23 doses of 7 vaccines. So, we've had a tripling of the numbers of doses of vaccines that children are now getting."[14]

Why do kids need 69 shots today? The cost of all these shots plus the cost of office visits can run up to $2500 in the U.S. Again, when my sister and I were kids none of these modern vaccines existed.

Although Fisher gave her kids the recommended doses she began to research whether this resulted in healthier children. In her book *A Shot in the Dark*, co-authored with Harris Coulter, Fisher documented the results of extensive research and analyzed various health concerns.

Are vaccinated children healthier in America?

Credit: http://amazon.com

"Just the opposite," Fisher explains. "We have an epidemic of chronic disease and disability. One child in six in America – now learning disabled. One in nine with asthma, one in 50 with autism, one in 400 is developing diabetes. Millions more have inflammatory bowel disorders, rheumatoid arthritis, and epilepsy."

But that's not all. She adds that, "30 percent now of young adults have been diagnosed as having a mental illness, anxiety disorder, bipolar, schizophrenia. This is the worst public health report card in the history of this country. And it has coincided perfectly with the tripling of the numbers of vaccines."[15]

The problems with vaccination policy today is an extensive and disturbing chronicle. Is the decline in young people's health really linked to the increased number of vaccines as Fisher proposes? That's the question we will examine next.

**Vaccine Efficacy**

Let's look at other examples to see if vaccines are as effective as health officials claim. In 2013 a mumps outbreak hit several American universities: Loyola University in Chicago, Fordham University in New York, and the University of Richmond in Virginia. By law, every college campus must have a 100% vaccination rate. So why were there outbreaks?

Credit: TTAV Global, LLC

Let's look at other states and other years. In 2016 the Cambridge Public Health Department reported an outbreak of confirmed mumps cases at Harvard University in Boston. On April 16, the Boston Globe reported that the number of cases had tripled since mid-March with 40 confirmed cases.

"This year's Harvard outbreak," the newspaper reported, "tops the last big mumps cluster in Massachusetts, when 39 confirmed and probable cases were recorded at Boston College in 2013."

The Globe article noted that at the beginning of April the CDC had 467 reported mumps cases nationwide, including mumps cases at Boston University, the University of Massachusetts Boston, Tufts University, Bentley University, as well as colleges and universities in other states.

Indiana health officials confirmed 22 mumps cases at Indiana University in Bloomington, 24 at Butler University in Indianapolis, five at Indiana University Indianapolis, and eight at Purdue University in West Lafayette.

Why didn't the vaccine protect all these students from the mumps? Clearly, vaccination doesn't provide complete and permanent protection.

Scott Zoback, spokesman for the Massachusetts health department said that the infected students were vaccinated against mumps, as required by law.

"It's possible the vaccine didn't work in some people," he declared, "or that the virus mutated in ways that made the shot less effective. The mumps vaccine fails to induce immunity in about 12 percent of people who receive it, so mumps outbreaks occur occasionally even in highly vaccinated populations."

But what about the herd immunity argument? In these cases, the idea of herd immunity was proven to be false. Even with a 100% vaccination rate among students, the disease struck showing that there was no herd immunity protection.

So now we know that the mumps vaccine doesn't work as marketed in at least 12% of cases. Is good money being wasted on a remedy that's not effective? Again, it was a failure of the vaccine not a failure to vaccinate.

Some health care professionals believe it's better for kids to get the mumps because it's a mild disease for children and then they have immunity for life. For young adult males, however, it's a much more serious disease, because it can affect the testicles and lead to sterility.

State health official Zobak quoted a figure that the vaccine fails in 12% of persons who get vaccinated. This figure means that 120 out of every 1000 vaccinated individuals will be unprotected.

### New York Times Report

In an early November 2017 article, "Mumps Makes a Comeback, Even Among the Vaccinated," the newspaper reported that vaccinated kids in the 18-22 age group are spreading mumps outbreaks. *"We are seeing it in a young and highly vaccinated population."* Yes, these are college students who have had the compulsory two doses of the mumps vaccine during childhood.

## Vaccine Verification

Most of the recent cases occurred in outbreaks, including a large outbreak in Arkansas, which goes to prove that the mumps vaccine doesn't work as promoted. Unfortunately, the *New York Times* is involved in the same quack understanding as the vaccine industry.

For example, they quote Dr. Patricia Quinlisk, the medical director and state epidemiologist for the Iowa Department of Public Health, who had to deal with an outbreak at the University of Iowa from 2015 - 2016 with more than 450 cases of mumps, who said that a decision was reached to **vaccinate students again.** Of course, with another **shot of the same vaccine** that failed to work the first time. [my emphasis]

Researcher Mike Adams explains an uncomfortable fact that vaccines which don't work "generate their own repeat business by not working." Yet doctors still claim that vaccines protect us from disease.

In order to rationalize why vaccines don't work, pharmaceutical companies fabricate the concept of booster shots. Because vaccination protection wears off, it needs to be repeated from time to time. Once again this generates more "repeat business by not working."

The real reason mumps vaccines, as well as others, don't work is explained in detail in Chapter Fourteen.

Of course, doctors inject the mumps dose as the MMR vaccine – a triple dose – which includes measles, mumps, and rubella. Does the same 12% figure apply to measles and rubella as well?

It would be important to know if your child is in the 12% group that vaccines fail to protect. How can you find out? You can't. No scientific studies have been conducted to discover what is the genetic nature of the 12% group.

Remarkably, no research has been done to determine why some individuals suffer adverse reactions from vaccines. Health officials still don't know what causes autism. The cause remains an enigma even though the science is there to find out the answers.

What is the difficulty to allocate funding for research that can improve our vaccine schedule? Why can't we make vaccines safer and more effective for every child?

We should be doing this, especially for kids whose genetic makeup reacts adversely to the present shots. Some kids cannot eat peanuts, others cannot eat soy. It's because of their genetics. Similarly, some kids cannot take 69 doses of vaccines.

The current one-size-fits-all approach to vaccination fails to recognize that children are not biologically identical. One of the primary principles of medicine is that no two persons are alike. Thus, every child must be diagnosed individually. Each child's immune response, overall health status, age, height and weight, is unique and it has to be taken into account.

The concept that the same concoction of chemicals can be given to every single child and expect no negative results, verifies that many doctors are in ignorance. Endorsing a one-size-fits-all vaccination for every infant nationwide is proof that something is drastically wrong with American healthcare.

Why is the topic of a child's individual genetic profile ignored to the point of forced vaccination?

In the opinion of Dr. Bob Sears, mandatory vaccination is a more important concern than herd immunity, which remains an untested premise.

"So the question is, are unvaccinated parents putting the rest of our children at risk? Maybe a little. But in my opinion," he explains, "parents SHOULD have the right to make health care choices for their children. They should not be forced into vaccinating if they feel strongly against it."

# ~ 4 ~
# Mandatory Vaccination

> The great enemy of the truth is very often not the lie
> – deliberate, contrived and dishonest – but the myth,
> persistent, persuasive, and unrealistic.
> Belief in myths allows the comfort of opinion
> without the discomfort of thought.
>
> - John F. Kennedy

In the last chapter, we asked if the decline in young people's health was linked to the increased number of vaccines as Barbara Loe Fisher alleged.

Journalist Amy Wallace doesn't think so.

"Before smallpox was eradicated with a vaccine," she writes, "it killed an estimated 500 million people. And just 60 years ago, polio paralyzed 16,000 Americans every year, while rubella caused birth defects and mental retardation in as many as 20,000 newborns. Measles infected 4 million children, killing 3,000 annually, and a bacterium called *Haemophilus influenzae type b* caused Hib meningitis in more than 15,000 children, leaving many with permanent brain damage. Infant mortality and abbreviated life spans — now regarded as a third world problem — were a first world reality."

Wallace always takes a pro-vaccine stance. Her article is sensational. She claims smallpox killed "an estimated 500 million people" before vaccines eradicated the disease. There are no records anywhere to verify that huge figure. It's her own estimation, plain and simple. When someone is new to the topic of vaccination they always start with smallpox, polio, and sensationalist figures.

Of course, many people do believe that vaccines have all but eradicated smallpox, polio, measles, mumps, and rubella. Therefore, this chapter will examine this belief in detail.

Is it true that a vaccine wiped out smallpox?

Renowned researcher and author, Dr. Sherri Tenpenny disagrees. "The truth of the matter is quite simply, no. By all estimations, less than 10% of the global population ever got vaccinated with the smallpox vaccine."

That means the 90% who weren't vaccinated were saved from smallpox by something other than the vaccine. Dr. Tenpenny explains.

"I went back in time and started looking at some old medical journals from the 1800s and early 1900s to try and identify the cause of death of smallpox. Was it infection, or secondary infection, lung disorder or

## Mandatory Vaccination

renal failure, kidneys shutdown? I had three different people help me to pour over all the old medical journals. We couldn't find anything significant."

Medical experts attribute improved sanitation and quarantine to smallpox eradication. Tenpenny agrees with that conclusion. She says that smallpox "went away by hygiene, toilets, clean water, and public health." But she wanted to get further confirmation from the leading authorities in the field.

In 2001 just after the events of 9/11, Dr. Tenpenny was involved with the CDC when they were having town meetings. She had concerns about how the evening news was urging people every night to revaccinate for smallpox when nobody knew if anyone could die from smallpox in the 21st century.

At one town meeting she was giving her reasons to the panel why it was unnecessary to re-vaccinate everybody.

"You say when smallpox was around there was a 30% death rate and after 9/11 they wanted to revaccinate all the doctors and first responders because there would be a 30% death rate. It was pounded into our heads on the 6 o'clock news every single night.

"We do not know what the cause of death was from smallpox. I can't find it anywhere. But we know for sure, that the last documented case of smallpox in this country was in Texas in 1940. How much farther have our medical technologies come since 1940 with antibiotics, antivirals, IV fluids, and any of those sorts of things. Is it really true that if someone contracted smallpox today that there would be a 30% death rate?"

There was no immediate answer to the question. But shortly after, Dr. D. A. Henderson, one of the head researchers for the smallpox eradication program in the 1980s, took up the microphone.

"That's a very good question," he said. "We really don't know. It's a mystery. We've looked at all the documentation and are quite sure it wasn't secondary infection. We're quite sure it wasn't renal failure. It may have been pulmonary but we really don't know. Historically, smallpox was spread worldwide as a filth disease, like typhoid and cholera, because unclean people spread the virus from person to person who didn't have a strong immune system against it."

At that same CDC town meeting a colleague of Dr. Henderson, Dr. Tom Mack, said that smallpox was on its way out anyway. It was going away because of hygiene, but went away a little faster because we instituted a smallpox vaccination program. He admitted that many eradication programs throughout India, China, and other countries, had the same data.

These two doctors were among the main people involved with smallpox eradication. One said we don't know what the cause of death was, and the other said it was already going away due to hygiene. Yet it's burned into our brains that a vaccine eradicated smallpox.

British doctor Vernon Coleman, MB, ChB, DSc, FRSA, candidly admits that, "One of the medical profession's greatest boasts is that it eradicated smallpox through the use of the smallpox vaccine. I myself believed this claim for many years. But it simply isn't true!"

The CDC has confirmed that the virulence of the smallpox virus becomes weaker over time. In fact, many viruses and bacteria come and go over time. Scarlet fever is a good example. Back at the turn of the 20th century, there were massive epidemics of scarlet fever caused by bacteria. Of course, that disease disappeared without a vaccine. So yes, viruses do come and go.

Next, let's examine the smallpox records so we can get more facts.

### Smallpox in the 19th Century

Historically, vaccinations follow the utilitarian philosophy of "what's best for the greater good." This was the rationale for England's mass smallpox vaccination in 1853. By 1857, fines and imprisonment awaited people who refused to be vaccinated.

According to the official figures of the Registrar General of England, between 1857 and 1859, there were over 14,000 deaths from smallpox. From 1863 to 1865, there were over 20,000 smallpox deaths.

Several years later, 1870 – 1872, there were almost 45,000 smallpox deaths.

Ironically, after England imposed mandatory smallpox vaccinations throughout the country massive epidemics began to occur. This flies in the face of conventional wisdom. Of course, the smallpox vaccine was developed long before we understood the human immune system.

Dr. Suzanne Humphries, PhD, is a renowned nephrologist who has studied the English smallpox outbreaks in great detail. She cites the case of Leicester.

The town of Leicester had a massive outbreak of smallpox in 1871. Even with a 95% infant vaccination rate they had the worst case in England. How could that be? Therefore, the townspeople were outraged when mandatory vaccination was introduced. They had lost faith because the vaccine hadn't curbed the disease.

To find a solution they organized a public rally, 80,000 people strong, which included local health officials and politicians. Thus, they opted to stop vaccinating. They reached a decision to implement stricter sanitation procedures as well as isolating every person who contracted the disease. Today we call it quarantine.

In the end, Leicester had the lowest death rate from smallpox compared to the nearby towns that were still vaccinating heavily. Dr. Humphries details the entire history of the English smallpox outbreaks in her book *Dissolving Illusions*.

The Leicester case study showed that superior sanitation and quarantine prevented the disease from spreading. It wasn't the vaccine. We eradicated smallpox with sanitation, clean and safe water treatment facilities, by replacing the stench of outhouses with flushing toilets, and all other major advances in public health policies and facilities. The advent of sewage treatment compared to open sewers was a huge factor in reducing disease.

The *World Health Statistics Annual*, 1973-1976, Volume 2, confirms the conclusion that vaccines did not eradicate disease. "There has been a steady decline of infectious diseases in most developing countries, regardless of the percentage of immunizations administered in these countries."

That statistic is from the '70s, so it's clear that the incidence of disease was waning before the influx of vaccines that began in 1989. Without a doubt, improved socioeconomic conditions have had a direct impact on disease reduction.

Better nutrition and less crowded living conditions have also reduced the transmission of disease. Lower birthrates have helped to decreased the number of susceptible household contacts.

The development of antibiotics and other treatments did increase survival rates among less healthy populations, but the effect of antibiotics has been steadily waning over the last few years.

When we look at tuberculosis at the turn of the 1900s, people died from it. They went to sanitariums, and everybody back then knew somebody who had been in a sanitarium for TB. But we didn't eradicate TB with a vaccine because we didn't have a TB vaccine.

There were no vaccines for bubonic plague, leprosy, yellow fever, cholera, or scarlet fever. Yet these diseases disappeared long before we invented vaccination. These diseases disappeared due to vastly improved living conditions, sanitation, and hygiene, as discussed above.

Yet vaccine manufacturers, and those who earn their livelihood from pharmaceutical companies, want to give the credit to vaccination so they can continue to profit from vaccine sales.

Now, let's take a look at the history of compulsory smallpox vaccination in the United States.

### Smallpox in America

When the state of Massachusetts enacted mandatory vaccination laws in 1855, smallpox epidemics continued to break out in 1859, 1860, 1864, 1865, and 1867, culminating with the infamous epidemic between 1872 and 1873. It was comparable to what struck England.

Similar events occurred in Ireland, Scotland, Holland, Germany, Sweden, Austria, Italy, and Japan during the late 1800s. As vaccination rates increased, so did the incidence of smallpox. Again, this defies modern conventional thinking.

As countries began implementing modern sanitation procedures the disease began to diminish. These events proved a direct correlation between sanitation/quarantine and smallpox. Yet pro-vaccine supporters only credit vaccination to stopping the disease.

What about polio? An analogous situation occurred with polio in the 1950s. When you look at the graphs, polio had already spiked and was going away before we introduced the vaccine in 1954. Morbidity and mortality was dropping before we used the vaccine.

But after we introduced the Salk vaccine there was a bump in the death rate. There was a bump in places that never even experienced polio. And we found a lot of this out from chiropractic journals. Chiropractors were seeing kids who had been vaccinated with the early injectable Salk polio vaccine, come in with lame limbs for treatment.

That's when the public health department changed the criteria for the definition of polio. Originally, polio was diagnosed if someone had an episode of paralysis that remained 72 hours after first being identified. But they changed the criteria. Now people had to have the paralysis two weeks later before they could be labeled as infected with polio. Other criteria began changing to make it appear that the vaccine was eradicating polio.

Remarkably, researchers in the '50s found that it was extremely difficult to inactivate the polio virus. Then they found that many people had contracted polio from the vaccine itself. This discovery prompted health officials to abandon the injectable polio vaccine and replace it with an oral vaccine. As with smallpox, the jab was not doing the job.

However, the oral vaccine also proved problematic. That's why the U.S. returned to using the injectable vaccine in the 1990s, but with an altered formula. Thus, the modern polio shot is unlike earlier versions that supposedly eradicated polio.

Although many countries use different strains of the polio virus in their vaccine, they neglect the correlation between sanitation and quarantine in polio's decline. It's a scientific fact that polio disappeared all over Europe and they didn't even use the vaccine!

In Canada, they stopped oral polio medication in 2001 when they found it was the only thing still causing polio due to the live viruses in the vaccine.

When we mention polio, people think of things like an iron lung, braces, paralysis. Even 60 years after the polio epidemic, those images are still shown. Yes, there were people who had polio and people who were paralyzed. Some were on an iron lung which was the precursor to the modern-day ventilator. Nobody thinks anything about people being on ventilators today. Our memory of polio is an American phenomenon.

Even the WHO stated that as long as we continue giving the oral polio vaccine globally, we will never eradicate the virus. Yet in Chapter Twelve, we find out that Bill Gates still pushes the oral polio vaccine to kids in India.

But wait a minute. Why is there a focus on eradicating a virus? We need to focus on eradicating paralysis. Although children in third world countries end up with paralysis, is it due to polio or something else? There are no studies so we don't really know the facts. The entire vaccination issue is a money-making business built mostly on fear.

### Eradicating Disease

The cause of almost every disease is due to unclean water, filthy latrines, and inadequate sanitation. Previously, there were no flushing toilets only stinking outhouses. There was no ER to get IV fluids. People died from diarrhea and dehydration, and still do in third world countries.

The WHO reported in 2016 that 10 out of the world's 20 most polluted cities were in India, based on residents' exposure to deadly small particulate matter. I have traveled to India and have seen garbage lying everywhere. Although there is a campaign for a cleaner India, there's only minor garbage cleanup. Most of it remains and festers month after month.

WaterAid, an international nonprofit group, determined that 70% of India's surface water is contaminated. In 2015 a government report found that 275 of the 445 rivers in India, including the Ganges, were severely polluted. Diarrhea, often caused by drinking bad water, is the fourth-leading cause of death in India, ahead of any cancer.

Disease is rampant in India due to open sewers, deadly particulate matter in the air that people breath, and the contaminated water they drink. Once India achieves a modern standard of hygiene and sanitation, disease will diminish drastically.

Vigorous sanitation schemes, clean water, and quarantine, stopped all major diseases before and will do so in future. The point is that we didn't vaccinate away disease.

Again, pharmaceutical companies don't want this to be public knowledge. They suppress negative reports because their products protect the livelihood of people working in the industry. It's why they always credit vaccines for stopping disease. That's fine for business, but it's not fine for health.

Even with the correlation to modern sanitation, the pharmaceutical industry contends that correlation doesn't prove causation.

## Mandatory Vaccination

Of course, if you're hit by a car nobody can deny that the car caused the injury. In this case, correlation proves causation. More interesting is when a person becomes ill after taking alternative medicine. Doctors quickly say the alternative treatment caused the illness. Again, correlation proves causation.

But if one suffers an adverse reaction after vaccination, they say the vaccine didn't cause the reaction. They will say the person was predisposed to that condition. It was only by chance that it happened after the vaccine.

Another major problem with the vaccination industry in terms of being a fear-based industry, is the false premises they drum into the public mindset:

1. Get vaccinated because everyone will contract a certain disease
2. If you're exposed, you absolutely will get sick
3. Unless you get the vaccine you're not safe
4. If you're vaccinated, you will not get sick

The above premises are false because:

1. Not everybody will contract a certain disease
2. Even if you are exposed you may not get sick
3. You can be vaccinated and still get the disease

We all know that infections come and go. Here's an interesting case study of a family with 6 kids. The 2 oldest were fully vaxxed, the 2 middle kids (7 & 8 years old) were partially vaxxed, the 4-year-old and 6-month baby were unvaccinated. The 2 older kids had a cough so they came in to get swabbed. Both had pertussis.

The doctor knew the baby was unvaccinated so he swabbed the whole family. Everybody was positive, including the baby who only had a runny nose. This case study showed that exposure doesn't always result in illness. Even if you're vaxxed, it doesn't prevent you from getting sick.

Assurances that vaccines are safe and effective won't stand unless the data supports the claim. We need long-term studies to say scientifically that vaccines are effective. The scientific method means asking uncomfortable questions. Researchers must follow every clue and accept data that may lead to a conclusion they might not like.

When science discourages questions, or removes unwanted data it's no longer science. It's dogma.

Dr. Suzanne Humphries claims that, "We have a highly profitable, lucrative religion that involves the government, industry, and academia. That religion is vaccination. People believe in vaccines. They'll tell you, they believe in vaccines. But you ask them what they know about vaccines and it will be almost nothing."

She explains that in the 21st century we still haven't assimilated a factual understanding of how the infant immune system works. By injecting vaccines into the tender bodies of infants you may "give them some short-term immunity, but you're also going to change their immune system so that it can't function the way it was designed to function."

# ~ 5 ~
# 20th Century Vaccine Law

> Immunizations not only did not prevent any infectious diseases, they caused more suffering and more deaths than has any other human activity in the entire history of medical intervention.
>
> - Viera Scheibner, PhD.

Let's research the historical cases that changed vaccine law in the U.S. We want to know why the laws were changed, who was responsible, and the legal ramifications of these modifications.

At the turn of the 20th century, the U.S. Supreme Court accepted that vaccination cured smallpox. Of course, the court did not consist of medical specialists, only legal authorities. As a result, the Jacobson v. Massachusetts 1905 ruling declared that the states have constitutional authority to employ police powers to enforce mandatory smallpox vaccinations.

Government determines what is legal and what is illegal via the court system. Pastor Jacobson went to court because he and his son had suffered severe reactions to earlier smallpox vaccinations. The case rested on his claim that he shouldn't have the vaccine due to an adverse genetic predisposition to it. This was the same point Dr. Healy made in Chapter One.

The Jacobson case finally arrived at the Supreme Court. The court ruled that the freedom of an individual can be subordinate to the greater good for the greatest number of people. It was another utilitarian decision. Therefore, the court ordered Jacobson to pay a $5 fee in lieu of receiving the smallpox vaccine. Since then courts have cited the 1905 Jacobson decision.

Of course, the United States of America was not founded upon utilitarian principles. It was founded on "the self-evident truth that all men are created equal, and endowed with unalienable rights of Life, Liberty, and the pursuit of Happiness."

To escape oppression, many people fled to America for liberty. So, the historical meaning of this passage was "no force."

Pro-vaccine advocates, like Amy Wallace and others, argue that vaccination is a public health issue. For the greater good of society government can suppress an individual's personal choice of life, liberty, and pursuit of happiness. Is this a valid argument?

The Fourth Amendment of the Bill of Rights affirms, "The right of the people **to be secure in their persons**, houses, papers, and effects, against unreasonable searches and seizures, **shall not be violated**..." [My emphasis]

"The right of the people to be secure in their persons" clearly refers to the plural not the singular. It means all people shall have the right to act according to their own belief system and that "shall not be violated."

Nobody can be forced against their religious belief, against their liberty or pursuit of happiness, which includes not taking certain medications that may have an adverse side-effect causing a person to lose life, liberty, or even to end pursuing happiness. That's the Constitution upon which the United States came into being.

America was founded on the principle of religious freedom and welcomed all oppressed people worldwide to come and practice their religion peacefully. Many vaccines contain animal products so for religions that emphasize vegetarianism, for example, the public health card is being used to trample upon that religious freedom.

Historically, adopting utilitarianism in support of public health, or any other policy, usually results in autocratic government. In the 1927 Buck v. Bell case, utilitarianism was the basis for the ruling.

The Supreme Court judged Carrie Buck, an unmarried Virginia mother and her child, to be mentally handicapped. Justice Oliver Wendell Holmes articulated the majority position for the court, affirming that compulsory sterilization of the unfit was acceptable. Thus, individual states could pass eugenics laws. Holmes stated, "three generations of imbeciles are enough."

That utilitarian decision gave a green light to Virginia and other states to pass eugenics laws that sterilized over 60,000 Americans, against their will, between 1927 and the mid-1940s. It's the American historical record.

The utilitarian principle, which upholds mandatory vaccination, is broad enough to cover the cutting of the fallopian tubes. I wonder if journalist Amy Wallace would accept the utilitarian standard if it applied to her own body.

After World War II, the states abandoned routine sterilization of people they considered genetically defective or a threat to the health of the state. Prior to that, however, eugenics was accepted as a genuine science to improve human population by controlled breeding and elimination of undesirables.

The eugenics idea originally came from Charles Darwin. He wrote that breeders of plants and farm animals always choose the best of each species for breeding purposes. He noted that we do not apply this practice in human society and this mistake continually degrades humanity. Hitler adopted Darwin's ideas to implement his master race plan.

## Human Rights Issues

When a country adopts a utilitarian rationale to promote public policy via compulsory vaccination, it's a very slippery slope. The utilitarian argument always seems to function when individual freedom is on the line. But that's not even the end of the story.

We need to examine the Nuremberg Code introduced in August 1947. This was an international legal agreement that two Americans helped to write. The Code was established to prevent, and forever avoid, forced medicine in any form including experimental medicine, which was rampant in Nazi Germany during World War II.

Credit: Public Domain photo

The Nuremberg Code has been hailed as a landmark document in medical and research ethics. The entire code is included in Chapter Sixteen.

The first and foremost point is that people involved in an experiment must give their informed consent.

Nobody can be forced to participate in medical experiments without understanding potential risks.

The code allows participants to leave a medical experiment if they so choose. Doctors must stop the experiment if they realize it may harm the patient. Today, it's clear that mandatory vaccination fits the category of forced medicine.

We can also rank vaccination as experimental medicine because vaccination is a medical procedure that lacks guarantees.

1. There's no guarantee that deliberate introduction of microorganisms into a healthy person will not compromise that person's health or cause untimely death.
2. There's no guarantee that the vaccine will protect the person from contracting a disease.
3. There's no adequate scientific knowledge concerning how vaccines singly or in combination interact with the body at the cellular and molecular level.
4. Medical science has not identified predictors to give advance warning that injury or death may occur.

Our children were guinea pigs for failed vaccines like DPT. That vaccine was taken off the market in the United States due to the huge public outcry against the adverse reactions it produced.

I interviewed a woman whose doctor advised her to vaccinate her first child with DPT. Anika remembers catching the tail end of a daytime program where a doctor had just told an audience ...*and that's why you shouldn't vaccinate your children.*

"I recall thinking I should make a mental note of it. Fast forward to 1989, and I had forgotten that mental note. Following my pediatrician's advice, I vaccinated my healthy, intelligent four-months young baby with the DPT vaccine.

"The doctor said she would be lethargic after the shot. She became very lethargic, and she stayed lethargic. In addition, her eyes would roll back. I asked my mom if this was normal.

"After the vaccination, my aunt-in-law, who was a nurse, came by and told us to take her to the doctor immediately, that this wasn't normal. I found out later that my daughter was having seizures.

"The neonatologist conducted an MRI which came back normal, although later MRIs showed damage. Then, an electroencephalogram (EEG) and a CAT Scan showed abnormalities. The doctor first diagnosed her with Hypsarrhythmia and Infantile Spasm. I was told to inject her with steroids for one month and my nine-months baby bloated up.

"Although, her Hypsarrythmia disappeared, she later developed gran-mal seizures, petite-mal and drop seizures. She had to wear a helmet after she lost a front tooth due to a violent drop seizure. She was also diagnosed with cerebral palsy (basically brain damage), Lennox Gaustaut Syndrome and autism. She was a perfectly normal child and after the DPT shot she developed all these unimaginable disorders!

"She became developmentally disabled. She couldn't even sit up without support until she was about the age of two. Now she is 28 years old and can't talk or walk. She can't feed herself or go to the bathroom, much less bathe herself. She is completely and totally dependent on me and my husband.

"Throughout the years we've tried all types of medications, diets, homeopathic, ayurvedic, naturopathic, even medicinal cannabis oil, but nothing works. Stem cells are our next option.

"The U.S. had a special arbitrary court set up for these types of cases, however, the cases that usually win are the ones where they took the child to the Emergency Room with 72 hours of the vaccine. We didn't fall in the 72 hours window, and based on that my daughter was not given any compensation.

"Throughout this ordeal, I realized how much modern medicine is simply a 'practice'... Doctors are still practicing and they do not know a lot. They're as much in the dark as we are."

Countless parents have had a similar experience as Anika by following the advice of their pediatrician to vaccinate a perfectly healthy baby.

## Individual Rights

Today we know that the DPT experiment failed, and was replaced by the DTaP vaccine.

Horrifying adverse vaccine side-effects caused the anti-vaccine movement. Unfortunately, the pharmaceutical companies continued using the old stock (they can hurt kids but not profits) before the supply was exhausted and no longer administered.

DPT is still a licensed vaccine in the U.S., but now it's shipped to other countries as a safe and effective American vaccine, except in America.

Award winning author and filmmaker, Dr. Leonard G. Horowitz is the world's most prolific, and most controversial, drug industry whistleblower. He publicly claims that "The greatest lie ever told is that vaccines are safe and effective." Clearly, the case of DPT vaccine and its use in third world countries corroborates the claim of Horowitz.

In another interview, Mark tells his story.

"I had an extremely bad reaction to a pharmaceutical called ciprofloxacin. There are thousands of people disabled by it. That was hands-down the worst experience I've ever had. Thankfully, I've mostly recovered over two years, but many people never do.

"When my arms were disabled and didn't work at all, the doctor would not admit the adverse reaction, even though it was printed on the side-effects insert. To him, it was anything but the drug that did that to me. And he wanted to catch me up on vaccines! That's when I discovered there's a huge movement of people – ex-vaxxers. The medical profession complicates the problems of life in their vain attempts to solve them.

"Some people will stop at nothing to convince others to inject themselves with the most disgusting contaminants. They don't care at what cost, or risk. To them., vaccines are forever safe and effective. Even when the evidence is right in front of their face, they won't accept it.

"It's sad because the molestation will start with heavy metal toxins before kids are even out of the womb. Watching kids have no childhood because of vaccines and Pharma assaults is the greatest problem for me. I prefer wild immunity than fake science by greedy, liability-free corporations.

"I'm getting hit with flu vaccine advertisements averaging three times a day. They are preying on people. They give the flu shot for free to get you into the hospital and sell you the Armani suit (chemo, more drugs, etc.)."

It's troubling to hear the stories of people who were harmed by Big Pharma drugs and vaccines which are promoted as safe and effective. Mandatory vaccination really is a Human Rights issue because forcing vaccination against one's will is anti-individual-rights.

Ultimately, the issue is about the personal use of one's own body. Mandatory vaccination actually boils down to three fundamental questions:

- Can I be forced to put things into my child's body against my will?
- Do I have a free choice to take care of my body, or my child's body?
- Can I be compelled to put chemicals into my body, or my child's body, unknowingly because the chemicals are not labeled?

The entire topic is one of the most fundamental issues to affect humans – health freedom. I compiled this book because I believe in individual human rights, and our country is at a tipping point right now.

What is mandatory vaccination really about if government decides what goes into your baby's body whether you like it or not? And to reinforce the point, unvaccinated kids will not get an education or child care benefits.

I don't know what other restrictions will be legislated down the road, but mandatory vaccination is not a positive step forward.

## Loss of Liberty

The liberty promised by democracy is gradually being withdrawn based on the rationale that it's for your own protection. The Patriot Act deprived Americans of certain freedoms, and by agreeing to give up their liberty people would be recognized as patriots.

"Give me liberty or give me death" was the battle cry of Patrick Henry, one of the great American patriots. This dictum led to the founding of the United States of America.

Henry delivered this speech at the Second Virginia Convention in Richmond on March 23, 1775. Two future U.S. Presidents were at that convention: George Washington and Thomas Jefferson. America was founded on the principle of individual liberty.

The vaccination issue is about you as an individual and your children as individuals for whom you are responsible. Mandated vaccines deprive you of your constitutional freedom to decide by your own choice what can be injected into your child's body.

Democracy means choosing what's best for you. If vaccination was so beneficial, who would refuse that benefit? It wouldn't be necessary to force people if the needle really protected everyone. Forcing people to take what they don't want is highly suspicious.

So, we all need to take a keen interest in this issue because it's about forcing a medical procedure on our children. Taking away your freedom to choose if you disagree makes this a human rights issue. The most fundamental human right is control of my own body and my baby's body.

# ~ 6 ~
# Childhood Vaccine Injury Act

> I am no longer trying to dig up evidence to
> prove vaccines cause autism. There is
> already abundant evidence...
> This debate is not scientific,
> but is political.
>
> - David Ayoub, M.D.

Under U.S. law prior to 1986, vaccine manufacturers were losing money due to the many lawsuits coming from vaccine injuries. The losses from compensatory and punitive damages ran into billions of dollars. The public began to view vaccines as unsafe.

The case that finally broke the camel's back was the 1986 Graham v. Wyeth decision. The jury awarded Michelle Graham $15 million because of the permanent neurological injury she received from the DPT (Diphtheria, Pertussis, and Tetanus) vaccine.

The decision was based on the fact that Wyeth Laboratories sold an unsafe product. Either knowingly or neglectfully, they lacked proper safety studies. Wyeth was also deficient in research to verify that DPT would not cause neurological damage to children.

Because of this ruling, all the pharmaceutical companies (Big Pharma) petitioned Congress with arguments to protect their business.

They claimed that:

1) They were losing money due to continued litigation
2) They needed to upgrade production facilities to make better vaccines
3) The capital to expand and upgrade was used to defend law suits
4) It made no sense businesswise to invest in a product and then get sued
5) A national security issue could result via an epidemic or a bioterrorism attack if they stopped making vaccines
6) There would be no production facilities to create new vaccines in response to a national emergency
7) If nothing is done, we'll have to stop making vaccines
8) You need to give us immunity from litigation

Congress felt obliged to protect the vaccine supply.

# Childhood Vaccine Injury Act

Their decision was based on the reality that the pharmaceutical industry was prepared to abandon vaccines altogether due to legal losses from vaccine-injured children. Emboldened by pharmaceutical industry money, Congress passed the National Childhood Vaccine Injury Act.

The Act gave all the vaccine producers total legal immunity from financial liability as part of a broad health bill favoring business concerns over children's health concerns. President Ronald Reagan reluctantly signed the bill into law on Nov 14, 1986.

Big Pharma hailed the legislation as a tremendous victory to allow them to stay in business. Vaccine litigation had proven to be not only costly and bad for business, but dreadful for their reputation. Now they had a flawless business model because they could no longer be sued for a defective product. This had never been done before, for any other industry.

Environmental attorney Robert F. Kennedy, Jr., explained it succinctly in an interview with Tucker Carlson on his news show April 20, 2017.

"So that no matter how sloppy the line protocols," Kennedy explained, "no matter how absent the quality control, no matter how toxic the ingredients, or egregious the injury to your child, you cannot sue them.

"So there's no depositions, there's no discovery, there's no class action suits. All of a sudden, vaccines became enormously profitable."

The immunity allowed pharmaceutical companies to avoid legal discovery, depositions, and the documentation that explores and scrutinizes the decision-making process of a company. Nobody can look at their books. Today's vaccine court does not allow any kind of discovery.

The vaccine regimen changed dramatically after the National Childhood Vaccine Injury Act became law. The newly unregulated pharmaceutical industry began to realize huge profits which encouraged manufacturers to produce new vaccines to inject into newborn children. The shots increased from 10 in 1986 to 69 today. It was like the Big Pharma gold rush as they began to add new and unnecessary vaccines to the spectrum.

Even if there were toxic ingredients, like aluminum or mercury, in the vaccines, and even when they seriously injured your child, nobody could sue them.

To provide protection for injured children some legal ruling had to counteract the no-accountability legislation favoring the vaccine industry.

The NVIC worked with Congress to include the Vaccine Adverse Event Reporting System (VAERS) in the 1986 health bill. This added provision made it compulsory for all doctors and health care providers to file a report of any adverse events following vaccination.

It would benefit children and adults by documenting adverse side-effects and provide safety provisions for every individual harmed by vaccination. The VAERS legislation also established a committee from the Institute of Medicine to review existing literature on vaccine adverse events, regardless of whether there was a direct link between events.

Another VAERS required provision was the Vaccine Information Statement (VIS). The VIS was a formal and concise description detailing the risks and benefits of each vaccine (as well as multi-dose vaccines). The law required doctors to give this information to families before injecting a vaccine into their children. The idea was that a parent would give their informed consent. The CDC had to distribute this information to state and local health departments as well as individual health providers.

The law further required every doctor to keep a permanent record of every vaccine and lot number that was administered. Moreover, whenever a vaccine caused a serious health problem, or injury, or hospitalization, a doctor had to keep that information with the patient's permanent medical record.

The 1986 legislation also launched the national Vaccine Injury Compensation Program (VICP) which later became known as the "vaccine court." The aim was to compensate persons of any age for vaccine injuries.

This program changed the entire civil compensation procedure by taking vaccine injury cases out of the courts. It was a special no-fault alternative to the traditional legal system. Now parents, legal guardians, and legal representatives could file a petition on behalf of children, disabled adults, even deceased individuals, who had a vaccine injury.[16]

These programs included in the 1986 Act were the unique contribution of the NVIC.

## Compliance by Doctors

Sadly, the reporting of serious vaccine health problems is not rigorous. The compliance rate is below 10%. Despite this appalling failure to report reactions, more than 25,000 adverse reactions are still reported to VAERS every year, including irreversible injuries and deaths.

It means that in 90% of cases countless children have suffered adverse reactions that were never reported. Non-compliance hinders the broadcast of data which prevents a parent from recognizing adverse reactions when they see them. It also hinders future prospects of improving vaccine safety and efficacy.

The requirements are rarely enforced because no penalties for non-compliance were stipulated. If you want, you can inquire from your doctor's office if they comply with the VAERS regulations.

## Childhood Vaccine Injury Act

Just for the HPV vaccine Gardacil alone, VAERS has logged 54,105 adverse reactions. Of these reactions, 7,418 were listed as "serious," 10,416 were listed as "did not recover," and 2,227 were listed as *"disabled."*

There were other VAERS listed reports which included 14,928 "emergency room visits after vaccination," 5,155 "hospitalized," 362 "deaths," and 868 "life-threatening."

Even more shocking is the coverup. A study by Harvard Medical School, which was funded by U.S. Health and Human Services, tracked a three-year period of VAERS reports from Harvard Pilgrim Health Care involving 715,000 patients. The study found that **"fewer than 1% of vaccine adverse events are reported."**

Moreover, a U.S. House Report stated: "Former FDA Commissioner David A. Kessler has estimated that VAERS reports **currently represent only a fraction of the serious adverse events.**"

When we utilize Harvard Medical School's findings of only one percent reporting, the recalculated VAERS HPV vaccine reports would be as high as 5,410,500 adverse reactions, with 1,041,600 disabled, and 36,200 deaths.

Due to the non-compliance mood of doctors, the NVIC wants all existing federal vaccine safety provisions to be codified into state law. This would enable

121

individual states to require pediatricians in their state to comply with safety regulations.

Among doctors who do report, however, most send their reports to the specific drug company, who then sends inferior quality copies to the FDA and CDC so those employees can't even use the reports to publish surveillance accounts on adverse reactions. It's a broken system, wherein the CDC and the Academy of Pediatrics can't do their job of warning doctors about adverse vaccine reactions.

The question many parents are asking is, do vaccine manufacturers ever consider that their vaccines are causing numerous adverse reactions?

It's unfortunate that healthcare officials do not listen to mothers who tell them about vaccine reactions. Doctors and pediatricians are in denial that they have injected a vaccine that harmed instead of protecting a child. Denial of vaccine-injury means ignoring evidence right under doctor's noses.

Despite the overall failures, VAERS has awarded $3.56 billion to vaccine-injured children since its inception until Dec 31, 2016. The payouts confirm that vaccines are not entirely safe, and adverse reactions are real. The CDC recognizes that vaccines do have adverse side-effects, but they continue to recommend 49 doses of 14 different vaccines for children before age six.

People are unaware that the HHS and the Department of Justice opposed the 1986 law. They claimed that if vaccination did cause injury or death, it's such a rare event that it's not measurable. They didn't want to acknowledge vaccine injuries and deaths because that would require compensation.

Of course, the $3.56 billion VAERS payouts proved them wrong.

## Freedom from Liability

At this point, another question has to be answered. Where does the money to compensate vaccine-injured children come from if vaccine manufacturers are immune from liability and cannot be sued?

The legislation that freed Big Pharma from legal liability consigned *their* liability on you, the parent. Most parents are unaware that the price of each vaccine shot includes an excise tax. Yes, every parent pays a tax for each vaccine they buy for their kids. This tax is deposited into a trust fund.

The money paid as compensation to children who suffer adverse vaccine side-effects comes from this fund. It does not come from the pharmaceutical companies. Once again, it's a tremendous benefit for the pharmaceutical industry because *you* have to pay when their product leads to an adverse reaction.

What were the other consequences of the 1986 legislation? Well, with a legal liability shield to protect them, vaccine producers began marketing more vaccines. After the Vaccine Injury Act, the number of doses increased dramatically from 10 in 1986 to 69 in 2016. Even if a vaccination harmed a child the vaccine company was not accountable for the injury.

## Thimerosal

Thimerosal is an antiseptic preservative that contains mercury. It was invented by the pharmaceutical company Eli Lilly & Co. and patented in 1927. Over time a vaccine serum goes bad, so thimerosal is added to vaccines because it's the cheapest preservative to give vaccines long shelf life.

It doesn't make a vaccine more effective because it's simply a preservative. But it means no loss of money from the serum going off, because doctors order large quantities to have ready stock for patients.

Before thimerosal's use as a preservative began, the rate of autism was 1 in 10,000. This figure remained for over 50 years. It was considered a rare disease. However, after 1989 when thimerosal became an ingredient in every vaccine, the autism rate increased to 1 in 500.

As more vaccines were developed, more thimerosal was being injected into children. In the early 2000s the rate jumped to 1 in 250. By 2007, the rate skyrocketed. Now 1 in 150 children became autistic. Five years later the figure soared to 1 in 88 by 2012.

In 2015, 1 in every 68 children became infected by autism. That translates to one million children in the

US diagnosed with autism. The latest autism figure estimated by scientists is 1 in 25 for 2018. That's considered to be a serious epidemic.

The youth of America has become severely compromised. Forget about going to college, it will be a miracle if these children learn to function as normal adults.

We all know that mercury is a substance we're not supposed to be exposed to. There are EPA warnings about eating certain types of seafood that contain mercury. It's among the most toxic elements known – far more toxic to the human body than lead.

The mercury content in vaccines is way above all mercury exposure guidelines. The EPA limit for mercury in drinking water is 2 parts per billion (ppb). The EPA classifies mercury at 200-ppb as the level in a liquid they classify as toxic, or **hazardous waste**.

The concentration of thimerosal in vaccines is 50,000-ppb. This amount is extremely toxic but that's how much they need to prevent the vaccine from spoiling. Long shelf life safeguards profits. When a product goes off, it must be disposed of resulting in lost money for the company.

The EPA guidelines are for methyl mercury, which is found in fish. Thimerosal is ethyl mercury, which is injected. That means 100% absorption, making it far more dangerous to our bodies because mercury is not fully absorbed by eating sea food.

From 1989 to 1992 the mercury content (thimerosal) in children's vaccines nearly tripled. And precisely at this time the epidemic of childhood disease began to occur.

For example. just how toxic is thimerosal in the multi-dose flu vaccine? The multi-dose flu shot has 25mcg of thimerosal/0.5ml. So, for 1.0ml that would be 50mcg, or 50,000mcg/liter, (1000ml = 1 liter).

Well, 1mcg/liter equals 1-ppb. Therefore, the flu shot has 50,000-ppb of thimerosal. The EPA safe limit for mercury in drinking water is 2-ppb. Mercury at 200-ppb is what the EPA considers a toxic hazard.

Clearly, the multi dose flu shot has 250 times more mercury than what's branded as a toxic hazard. Compare the 200-ppb figure to the 50,000-ppb concentration of mercury in thimerosal, which gives the flu shot serum long shelf life.

Even more disturbing is when a doctor accidentally drops a vial of flu vaccine and it breaks. By law he is required to call in a hazmat (hazardous materials) team to clean it up and dispose of it as hazardous waste. It can't be put into a garbage can. He also has to evacuate the building because the mercury in thimerosal is toxic to people nearby.

Yet we inject that amount into our kids and pregnant women? It makes no sense! It's a bad idea. Young children are the most vulnerable. And if it's early in the pregnancy, which is recommended under the current advisories, that tiny fetus could be getting thousands of times more mercury than what the EPA claims is safe for adults.

Regardless of your position on the flu vaccine, the amount of thimerosal in the flu shot is alarming.

Due to the public outcry against mercury, vaccine manufacturers say only "trace amounts" of thimerosal remain, which are not harmful to the body. Chapter Fourteen takes an in-depth look at the so-called "trace amounts" of mercury toxicity in vaccines. The actual truth will be a shock to parents.

Although most people never read the science, or analyze the claims, they swear that science has exonerated mercury from any involvement with autism. But just ask them, *what study are you talking about?* They cannot name a study they have read. It's alarming that people can be so ignorant and so vocal at the same time.

There are hundreds of studies showing how thimerosal is destructive to brain tissue. Many studies have found a link between mercury and autism. These studies cite mercury damage in test animals, as well as in humans.

Attorney Robert F. Kennedy, Jr. tells us that a tremendous gap exists between the public perception of mercury and autism. There's an even larger gap between what the actual scientific studies show, and the government's characterization of the science. He says there's a rich scientific literature that anybody can access on PubMed.

You may well ask, why is there such a disconnect? Who are these persons who deny the mercury link and what is their purpose?

There are numerous factors, so here's a few just for starters. First, as stated earlier a huge amount of money comes to media as revenue from advertising. Six major corporations control all newspapers, TV stations, radio stations, and most internet content providers in the U.S. The majority of their ad revenue, over 70%, comes from the pharmaceutical industry. That's why the press is in denial.

You don't bite the hand that feeds you. Anti-vaccine coverage in the media harms ad revenue, so they don't cover the vaccine issue, even though this contravenes journalism ethics and exposes journalistic malpractice.

Second, journalists, reporters, and editors believe they perform a critical public health function by encouraging increased vaccination. They think that allowing debate on vaccine safety is detrimental to public health because people will stop vaccinating, which, to them, means killing kids.

Pharmaceutical companies, who pay the ad revenue, drill this mantra into media employees: anti-vax = kids die. Is this a fact? We need exploration and studies before this premise can be accepted as fact, but such studies are not being done.

However, we live in a democracy where people do have a choice. We must continue to uphold the freedom of choice guaranteed in our Constitution and Bill of Rights.

The Patriot Act has already started to whittle away our liberty. The Act has set a dangerous precedent by taking away people's freedom to choose. What's next?

Throughout the 1990s and into the turn of the century, shabby science continued support for vaccination. Even though most vaccines are laced with aluminum and thimerosal, the pharmaceutical liability shield continued to protect industry.

Nevertheless, attorneys representing injured children were still successfully suing vaccine manufacturers by proving that a safer vaccine could be made.

Once again, pharmaceutical companies were losing money defending lawsuits.

## ~ 7 ~
# Unavoidably Unsafe

> You can fool all the people some of the time,
> and some of the people all the time, but
> you cannot fool all the people
> all the time.
>
> - Abraham Lincoln

In 2011 another DPT injury case against Wyeth Laboratories arrives at the Supreme Court. In the 25 years since the Graham v. Wyeth ruling, the DPT vaccine formula has remained the same despite the many adverse side-effects that have harmed children.

Now in Bruesewitz v. Wyeth, trial lawyers arguing for Big Pharma, government, and the medical industry, convinced the Court that the pharmaceutical industry should have no liability *if* the Federal Drug Administration (FDA) licensed vaccines as safe and effective.

In other words, the responsibility for vaccine safety now fell upon the shoulders of the government agency. Although the female Justices, Sotomayor and Ginsburg, dissented, the Supreme Court majority ruled that, "Vaccines are unavoidably unsafe and there shall be no more lawsuits against any vaccine company."

That's how it stands today. Every vaccine is legally classified as "unavoidably unsafe." It means that legally no one can avoid the reality that vaccines are unsafe. This closed the loophole that allowed persons harmed by vaccines to sue for medical malpractice.

The 2011 legislation gave a tremendous benefit to Big Pharmaceutical companies, which was what they had lobbied for. But, one question remains. *If the pharmaceutical industry is free from all liability, who would be held accountable when a vaccine injured a child?*

Barbara Loe Fisher explains the hidden meaning. "Today, if you or your child are injured by vaccine, or if your child dies from a vaccine, you cannot hold anyone accountable in a civil court of law – anyone who makes or sells the vaccine, who regulates the vaccine and who makes policy for the vaccine, who votes to mandate for the vaccine, or who gives the vaccine. The only one who's left with any responsibility for what happens to a child after that child is injured by a vaccine, is the parent."

The 2011 ruling thrust all the risk from any adverse vaccine reactions, including autism, upon the parents. Nobody else in the vaccine business takes a risk because they have absolute immunity. There is no reason to invest money for liability insurance, quality control, or trial lawyers, due to the absolute immunity shield.

No other industry has a deal like this with blanket immunity from liability. The nuclear power industry does have limited indemnity but not like the pharmaceutical industry, which does an annual business of $30 billion. So the incentives to get a vaccine on the schedule is enormous with no liability forever. No other product can return such benefits to a company.

What if you couldn't sue a car company when their brakes failed? Imagine buying a car with defective brakes. When the brakes fail, you can't sue, so there's no financial loss for the company. It's a foolproof business model.

To keep industry honest, law suits are necessary. They protect consumers. What about the many side-effects that have injured kids? Drug companies are not concerned with side-effects. They list them on the insert in every package for their own legal protection. The printed insert warns users of potential side-effects. If you choose to disregard the warning and suffer a serious side-effect, you have nobody to blame but yourself.

When a vaccine contributes to injuries, autism, cancer, or destroys the life of a child, nobody else is liable except the parents. That's because vaccines are legally "unavoidably unsafe."

It's now clear that the vaccine industry is a shallow, narcissistic, heartless business.

If the legality of the vaccine business is that only a parent is liable in case of an adverse reaction, shouldn't parents be allowed a choice not to vaccinate?

One time my wife suffered from severe stomach pain and I had to rush her to the ER. The hospital had a doctor examine her. He advised a certain medicine, which I immediately purchased. When we read the side-effects on the insert, they were far worse than the pain she was experiencing. My wife decided not to take those tablets. After a good night's rest, she felt a lot better, and we checked out of the hospital leaving the tablets behind.

==We exercised our choice not to take the medicine,== and ==nobody objected. With vaccines we have no choice. Why the double standard?==

Health officials continually challenge parents of vaccine-injured kids, *where's the proof it was the vaccine*? Regrettably, it's almost impossible to track symptoms and side-effects to the source. A parent must be prepared for possible adverse reactions.

Who wants to play this game with health officials who are in denial?

All persons own their body and should be free to make decisions for its wellness. Democracy doesn't mean my body is the property of the state.

Compulsory medical intervention via vaccination is an abrogation of the Nuremberg Code.

## Healthcare as a Business

For families with a vaccine-injured child the Supreme Court ruling was proof that vaccines were unsafe, indeed unavoidably unsafe. On the other hand, the fact that vaccine manufacturers now have absolute legal immunity is heartbreaking.

Every company knows that repeat customers are the basis for a successful business. This is what Business Administration courses teach. Repeat customers in the medical field means sick people. Healthy people are no longer customers.

Credit: bizzaro.com

Vaccine-injured children will have to rely on doctors, hospitals, and medications for the rest of their lives.

Big Pharma no longer has any fear of retribution from the increased number of shots given to children – 10 in 1986, 69 in 2016.

Indemnifying vaccine makers, due to so-called public health benefits, have given companies increased profits. They don't have to spend money for long-term safety trials. There are no long-term studies for the life-span of an individual. Vaccine studies are only for short-term immediate safety.

Companies now reinvest profits into developing vaccines for diseases that are not fatal, just inconvenient. It's a troubling factor because the consequence is a reduced public health benefit in terms of child mortality.

Nowadays the pharmaceutical lobby has become so powerful that it is dictating federal policy on vaccinations, which they have relabeled as immunization. Recent legislation has benefited the pharmaceutical industry greatly while at the same time reducing the public's health freedom. This legislation has set a terrible precedent.

Now other multinational corporations are using the same strategy as the vaccine lobby to benefit their business at the expense of the public. In Germany the automobile industry claimed they couldn't upgrade their factories to the clean technology of electric cars due to the extreme cost of conversion. They threatened to take their factories to other countries unless there was legislation to favor the old combustion engine technology.

What other benefits have vaccine companies derived from legislation? They no longer need to do compulsory double-blind studies, which are necessary for drugs. Current law does not classify vaccines as drugs. Hence, vaccines have a streamlined process of approval with little scrutiny for safety or quality control.

No other product sold to the public has the same kind of protection and ease of approval. Due to the pharmaceutical lobby in Washington, legislation has transformed vaccines into an enormously enhanced product:

- government mandated for every child living in the country
- free from all risk due to being "unavoidably unsafe"
- parents pay liability for adverse side-effects by a tax

Except for the vaccine industry, no other business can legally produce and offer products or services without liability insurance.

Once a vaccine is approved, the following benefits apply to manufacturers:

1. A massive marketplace that must use your product

2. Kids have to get vaccinated, or they're denied an education
3. Complete protection from liability in case of damages
4. The end user pays all damage costs by a vaccine tax
5. No welfare benefits to pay out to anyone

The manufacturer has no down-side. Pharma has reached the Capitalist Imperative.

The health care system has become big business with huge profits. Lobbyists influence politicians to draft legislation that favors business, not health. Recent legislation has created a system that cuts corners.

The only catch was to get new vaccines approved. Lobbyists approached doctors at the CDC and FDA to fast-track vaccine approval. Now, an extraordinary fast-track situation, which does not exist for drugs, functions for vaccines.

When the existing product is free from liability, makes good money, and the government adopts mandatory immunization for the entire population, there's no incentive to develop an improved vaccine. Nothing is driving product improvement.

Every business decision is made to avoid losing or wasting money. It's costly to conduct adequate studies prior to introducing a vaccine. Thus, inadequate safety studies allow new vaccines to be licensed without proper oversight.

Vaccine producers don't look to the future to analyze long-term effects. Their focus is the next quarter. If shareholders are happy, it's business as usual.

## Vaccination is now Immunization

Vaccination means: to inoculate with the modified virus of any of various diseases, as a preventative measure. This is what people experience – being injected with a vaccine to prevent disease.

Immunization is defined as: the condition that permits either natural or acquired resistance to disease; to render harmless or ineffective; to neutralize.

Natural immunity means a person is immune from a specific disease for life. Acquired immunity is actually vaccination, which is not for life. Booster shots are required to boost the acquired immunity because it wears off. Natural immunity doesn't wear off.

Acquired immunity is the preferred choice of pharmaceutical companies because they can continue to sell booster shots. However, they prefer the term immunization, which has the connotation of natural immunity. Chapter Fourteen examines the dramatic difference between immunization and vaccination.

Clearly, vaccination is associated with acquired immunity, which is qualitatively inferior to natural immunity. This means that using vaccines to prevent natural exposure to mild pathogens may not be best for your child.

Vaccines, flu shots, and drugs continue to harm some persons and cause others to develop chronic ailments. Risky side-effects are keeping children weak and unhealthy. All drugs and vaccines have side-effects. This justifies the view that Big Pharma is selling sickness because nothing benefits a business better than repeat customers.

**Child Protection**

Despite the complete lack of corporate ethics, is there an existing government institution that survives to benefit the children?

Let's take a good look at the Vaccine Adverse Event Reporting System whose mandate is to compensate children for vaccine injuries. Most pediatricians and media people are unaware that VAERS even exists. Due to a lack of knowledge, they foolishly claim, *vaccines are safe and effective.*

I don't know why doctors claim that vaccines are safe and effective when, a) the Supreme Court has already ruled that vaccines are "unavoidably unsafe" and, b) VAERS has awarded $3.56 billion to vaccine injured children. The payout proves them wrong. What more proof do people need that vaccines have harmed so many kids?

Does your pediatrician even know about the VAERS compensation program? Although that program is kept quiet, it was originally intended to be widely distributed. However, the information is available on the U.S. Department of Health and Human Services website so you can see for yourself.

I think it's clear that every parent needs to evaluate the risks and benefits of vaccines before agreeing to inoculate their kids. How many more children must we harm before a huge outcry forces an investigation and a genuine change in vaccine policy?

Dr. Paul Thomas discussed this topic in an interview with medical researcher Ty Bollinger.

**Dr. Thomas:** "As a pediatrician, you're trained to believe that the CDC is the top. NIH and CDC are the top institutions where all the smartest people are. And so, we just accepted what they fed us without questioning. That's where I was when I got out of medical school, and that's where I was for the first few years of my practice.

"That all changed in 2001 when they pushed the Hep B onto newborns, because it made no sense. It is scientifically illogical, and absolutely insane, to inject that much toxin into a baby who doesn't even get any protection from the vaccine."

The Hep B vaccine Dr. Thomas is talking about was designed to give protection from sexually transmitted diseases. Infants won't have sexual relations for more than a decade after the shot. Many doctors agree that giving a newborn infant a Hep B shot on day one of life is inexplicable.

Even more disconcerting is that the Hep B vaccine is loaded with aluminum. Every one of those billion aluminum atoms in the serum can damage a fragile newborn body.

Factually, there are studies with data over 20 years that proves the Hep B doesn't even give lasting immunity. All studies show that vaccinations only give temporary protection because immunity wears off. That's why vaccines always need booster shots.

**Dr. Thomas:** "So when they need it most, when they're sexually active as late teens, 20s, they don't have the protection. That was when my blind faith in the CDC just went out the window and I started thinking, there's something going on here. People who worked at very high levels in the CDC end up working for Pharma."

The question arises at this point whether the CDC itself has been compromised. Its mandate is to be responsible for establishing a safe childhood vaccine schedule. But we are finding out that the CDC holds patents on multiple vaccines. These blatant conflicts of interest have been documented.

When we do a patent search, we can easily see that the CDC is listed as an assignee on more than 50 patents related to vaccines. These include flu, rotavirus, Hep A, HIV, anthrax, rabies, pneumococcal, meningococcal and several other vaccines. The CDC has a financial interest to increase the number of people receiving shots.

Dr. Brian Hooker, PhD, is a science advisor who has studied the experience of former CDC employees who end up in industry.

**Dr. Hooker:** "Dr. Julie Gerberding, who was the director of the CDC from 2001 until 2008, took a very lucrative position as the head of the vaccine division in Merck in 2009. She was given stock options in the millions for that particular position. Overnight she became a millionaire."

There are other employees that have gone on to lucrative positions in the pharmaceutical industry that Hooker has documented.

**Dr. Hooker:** "There's actually a revolving door between the CDC and the vaccine industry. Dr. Thompson himself came from Merck. He worked at Merck before he worked at the CDC. Dr. Frank DeStefano, who is the current head of the Immunization Safety Office at the CDC, actually left the CDC went into industry and then came back to the CDC. They are a risk management organization. And they are there to basically produce studies that will sway the opinion towards what CDC wants the public to do. And that is to uptake all the vaccines that they're recommending on the schedule."

The CDC doesn't appear to be a public health agency making independent safety recommendations by any stretch of the imagination. It looks a lot more like an incestuous relationship between the pharmaceutical industry and the CDC.

**Dr. Hooker:** "So really the driver is money. You know, it's just like everything else; the driver is the almighty dollar. And when an individual, which could be a CDC employee, gets a vaccination on the schedule that opens up a market for that particular vaccine, that's in the billions of dollars!"

Well, it's abundantly clear now. Big Pharma benefits tremendously when one of their vaccines is put on the CDC schedule because it translates into billions of dollars of sales year after year. And the CDC also profits because they are a patent holder.

And now the CDC has authorized the HPV shot on day one for newborns. Two shots injected into infants on the first day of their life? This has never been done since the dawn of time. But it's worth billions of dollars yearly, so it is a good business decision.

I think we can all agree that it's a serious disconnect to inject a vaccine into newborns for protection against sexually transmitted diseases they won't encounter for many years. Moreover, the vaccine antibodies normally last only 3-5 years. By the time these kids become sexually active, they'll have already lost that protection.

So why are newborns getting vaccinated on the first day of life? It makes no logical sense unless there's an underlying agenda that is being kept hidden.

CBS News recently reported that more infants die on the first day of life in the United States than all other industrial nations combined. How is that possible? Well, on their first day of life when newborns are literally gasping for their first breaths, we inject them with vaccines for protection against sexually transmitted diseases. Welcome to America!

How safe are these shots for newborns? It's illegal to test on newborn infants. Therefore, no testing for safety would have occurred before giving these shots right after the birth of your baby. ==Unfortunately, HPV is too new to see results of studies, so there's no long-term data on this vaccine.==

It's another huge disconnect because no scientist can possibly explain how multiple vaccines throughout infancy and early childhood affect a baby's developing brain and physiology.

Why risk damaging your child's developing brain and immune system? It may lead to increased risk for immune and brain disorders. Let others take that risk if they so choose. For anything new, I always prefer to err on the side of caution.

Who is allowing this to happen to innocent newborns? It makes no sense at all, except if some big shots are lining their pockets. It only makes business sense from a profit perspective. And that thought is disturbing.

### Government Agencies

Society has established several institutions to protect children's health:

First is the FDA. Their job was to affirmatively prove vaccines were safe and effective before giving a license to market. The DPT scandal proved they were derelict in their duty.

Second is the CDC. Their job was supposed to ensure all licensed vaccines were based on safety, efficacy, and need. The growing number of vaccine-injured kids prove they have been derelict in their duty.

The third group to protect kids is The American Academy of Pediatrics and pediatricians. Allowing the inclusion of aluminum and mercury in vaccines prove they have been derelict in their duty.

The fourth group to protect children from disease was the pharmaceutical industry. Because they can no longer be sued for an unsafe product, they are off the hook. They have placed profits ahead of kids which proves they are derelict in their duty.

Every group that was established to protect children has failed. Some people have said they can't believe this is going on in twenty-first century America. Others find it difficult to believe that health officials can be corrupted to this extent. So, let's look at the reality of the situation.

When you work for a drug company or a government health agency, you're paid a large salary. You're encouraged to upgrade to a fine home in the best part of town. They want you to enjoy a luxury lifestyle with the best house, car, or even a yacht. It's for prestige, to show your success in life. It sounds good from the employee perspective.

From the company's perspective, they want you to make large monthly payments to support your luxurious lifestyle. Why? Because you become dependent on making regular payments. If you question company policy, you risk losing your job. When you can't continue making payments your house and car will be repossessed, and your credit rating tanks. Your life comes crashing down and family and friends will turn on you.

It means you must tow the party line because employees are expendable. You have no choice but to keep quiet because you've become a debt slave to the corporation.

But what if you're sure the company is doing something wrong? If your conscience bothers you, the only option is to become a whistleblower and sneak out the evidence. But that's extremely difficult because companies have built systems to protect proprietary information.

You finally realize that it's best to keep quiet so your family continues living the good life, and your kids go to the best universities. You have been purchased and you may hate yourself, but at least you still have the respect of friends and family.

The drug companies are calling the shots – for employees and for the public. They have us believing propaganda for which there is no evidence. For instance, if we prevent the virus, we prevent the cancers later on. But there's no proof that it's true; no long-term studies to validate that conclusion.

Viruses and bacteria have been around forever, so they know how to adapt and mutate to stay a step ahead of any vaccine we come up with. The answer is not at the end of a needle, or at the bottom of a pill bottle.

The answer is in a healthy immune system. Over millions of years the human body has developed a strong immune system that's far superior to any vaccine because it can handle any bug thrown at it. Moreover, it's not even about the bug; it's about the host.

Many years ago, Antoine Bechamp, as well as Weston Price, wrote about this principle that the health of the host has the most power. The disease has the least power. The host wins when we keep the immune system strong.

## The Health Transformation

Eventually, the health paradigm will shift from a drug and vaccine standard to a model that embraces a more open and natural way of staying healthy. Drug companies and health officials who are committed to the old standard, fear a paradigm shift because they may lose market share. They're afraid of losing money.

I see more and more people experiencing health transformations, avoiding vaccines, and steering clear of drugs. It's about reducing exposure to toxins, paying attention to the quality of the food we eat, and exercise. People are becoming more aware, and change is happening.

Today the public learns from the internet and social media. Business models have already begun to pay attention, and the pharmaceutical industry will also have to respond. They may resist or adapt quickly. Nobody knows how they'll respond, but as long as we have the internet, the health transformation will continue to grow as we share with our family, friends, and co-workers.

From the evolutionary perspective, nature employs sunshine, clean air, clean water, nutritious food, and a strong immune system, for disease protection. Humans have lived strong and healthy throughout the ages, and we can credit that survival to a strong immune system, not to the use of vaccines.

We want to achieve long-term good health in society – individually and collectively. Everybody needs to take a deep breath, embrace innovative initiatives, and welcome dialogue because the goal is good health. Of course, it depends what side of the fence you're on. If the goal is to increase profits, who can imagine what Big Pharma will do?

Why should I trust people I don't know and blindly accept what they say is true? I choose to protect my children from all risk as their birthright.

The bottom line is that a parent can no longer trust other people with their children's health. Every parent must now take full responsibility to protect their kids. That should begin by studying the product insert that lists ingredients and side-effects before choosing to vaccinate. To jab kids with a syringe full of unknown chemicals because you didn't bother to read the vaccine insert is irresponsible.

If your pediatrician tries to dismiss your concerns, or pushes you to vaccinate, you may need a new doctor. By law, doctors are required to explain the insert and answer questions. Any other behavior is unacceptable.

If we continue to use vaccines, what can we expect to see in the next generation? We are experiencing an entire generation of children growing up damaged after being vaxxed. Most of these kids won't be able to work as adults, so they'll need to be institutionalized.

That means tax dollars supporting them. Will the government provide them with food, shelter, and medical care? How will this affect the financial burden to society?

Even more disturbing is *who will love them*? Statistics show that autism will affect your family, if not directly, then indirectly. If not now, then later because who will care for vaccine-injured kids when they're adults and when their parents become infirm or die? It's tearing families apart, and it will affect everyone.

We're at a tipping point. The question is how our vaccine mistakes will impact future generations? We must deal with this right now.

When science looks back on our current vaccination schedule fifty years from now, it will be clear we made mistakes. Our vaccine science is not perfect, and from the 2068 perspective, our errors will appear catastrophic.

But worst of all, the entire mess is being covered up. The media will never touch these stories because they risk losing revenue from pharmaceutical ads. But what about the children? How will newlyweds deal with the vaccine issue for their kids in the coming years?

# ~ 8 ~
# Supreme Court Fallout

> Only after realizing that routine immunizations were dangerous did I achieve a substantial drop in infant death rates.
>
> - Archie Kalokerinos A.A.M., M.B.B.S., PhD., F.A.P.M.

The question that might be running through your mind now is *why does legislation always favor Corporate America at the expense of everybody else*? In this chapter we will examine this issue as well as the repercussions from the Supreme Court decision that all vaccines are "unavoidably unsafe."

According to the U.S. Constitution, whatever is *not* defined as a matter for the federal government automatically defaults to the state governments. As a result, both public health laws and vaccine laws are statutory. They are created by each individual state, not by the federal government. That's why each state has different vaccine laws and different vaccine exemptions.

Previously all fifty states used to offer a medical exemption, while forty-seven states gave a vaccine exemption based on religious belief. Today we are losing these legal rights of vaccination choice. The result is that pediatricians are injecting more kids with more vaccines.

Pro-vaccine proponents argue that nobody should have freedom to refuse vaccinating, even in a democracy. They use the compulsory seatbelt law to validate their argument.

Again, it's the common false analogy argument. On one hand, there are no adverse side-effects from wearing a seat belt. There is only a benefit.

On the other hand, pediatricians must record any adverse side-effects from giving vaccinations. By law, doctors must send these records to VAERS. The VAERS program has already paid out billions in compensation to children injured by vaccines.

Fear of getting a disease is a risk many people believe can be minimized by vaccination. But that's a medical choice, and every person has a right to choose what goes into their body. That's why the Nuremberg Code exists.

A choice is always available in a democracy, but not in a dictatorship where individual choice is undermined.

## Double Standard

Despite the 2011 Supreme Court ruling that vaccines were "unavoidably unsafe," by 2014 the pharmaceutical industry implemented a massive campaign to convince the public that vaccines *were* safe.

The following announcement originally on CNN, was broadcast on all major TV stations and newspapers, and appeared in many countries.

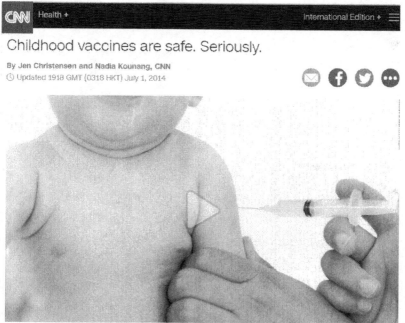

Credit: photo illustration/thinkstock

Vaccine companies spent a massive amount of money to convince the public that vaccines are seriously safe despite their legal classification as "unavoidably unsafe."

Remarkably, while drug companies remain protected from all liability because vaccines are unavoidably unsafe, they stick it in the face of that ruling by advertising, "Childhood Vaccines are Safe. Seriously."

By promoting the exact opposite reality worldwide, Big Pharma can now get the benefits of both safe and unsafe.

On the Fox News website, a follow-up article to the "Childhood Vaccines are Safe" ad boldly announced, "Children should get vaccinated against preventable and potentially deadly diseases. Period."

The article cites a report from the medical journal *Pediatrics* that a review of over "20,000 scientific studies on childhood vaccines" determined that "side effects from vaccines are incredibly rare." Thus, they concluded that all childhood vaccines are *safe*.

No mention in the article of the $3.56 billion payout to vaccine injured kids. Ironically, most of the 20,000 studies were the same studies that the Supreme Court analyzed to conclude that vaccines were "unavoidably unsafe."

It's more obvious than ever before that our children are now the battlefield where the war for corporate profits is being waged. At face value, business decisions are making our children a market place for the pharmaceutical industry.

The Fox News article quoted pediatrician Dr. Ari Brown, author of a popular book *Baby 411*. "Vaccines, like any other medication, aren't 100% risk free." Of course, by avoiding a shot, vaccines are 100% risk free.

By mistake, Dr. Brown weakened the claim that childhood vaccines are seriously safe because the article listed problems with vaccines that were definitely not risk free.

"There was evidence that the meningococcal vaccine can lead to anaphylaxis — a severe, whole-body allergic reaction — in children allergic to ingredients in the vaccine. A study of the polio vaccine found that children with atopic dermatitis and a family history of allergies did have a higher chance of developing sensitivity to food allergens. Other studies found the MMR vaccine was linked to seizures."

One of the problems referred to was, "children allergic to ingredients in the vaccine." Also, "studies found the MMR vaccine was linked to seizures."

Who wants to gamble with giving these potential risks to their kids? In Chapter Fourteen we examine the ingredients in most vaccines. You will understand why a youngster's body would be allergic to such ingredients. Again, avoiding the vaccine means no allergic reaction to the ingredients.

Most pediatricians must be unaware that the vaccines they dispense to children under their care are legally "unavoidably unsafe." Otherwise they wouldn't indiscriminately give your child all 69 shots on the CDC schedule. Or would they?

The 2011 Supreme Court ruling protected all persons who dispensed vaccines from liability for any side-effects resulting from vaccines they inject. Yes, your pediatrician has total immunity from liability if your child is harmed.

Bestselling author Robert F. Kennedy, Jr., is a trained environmental attorney. His book *Thimerosal* details the evidence for the necessary removal of the ethyl mercury ingredient used in vaccines, which some young bodies would naturally be allergic to.

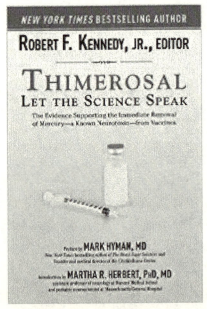

Credit: http://amazon.com

## Supreme Court Fallout

Is thimerosal no longer an ingredient in vaccines? That's what we're told by the CDC. In Chapter Fourteen we examine the shocking evidence.

Kennedy tells us that when he was a kid, "I got smallpox vaccine and I got polio vaccine and that was it. My kids received 69 doses of 16 vaccines."

He only got two shots when he was a child because that was normal back then. He can't be labeled anti-vaccine if he gave every dose on the CDC schedule to his kids. Yet, he's upset because he believes people have a fundamental right to freedom of choice. That's why he is opposed to mandatory vaccination.

### Kickback Scheme

Moreover, he says he's disturbed that insurance companies like Blue Cross Blue Shield punish doctors financially if they don't acquire a certain percentage of patients following the CDC vaccine schedule. What is that percentage?

"If 63% are not complying," he explains, "they don't get any of their bonuses. If a pediatrician does not persuade his patients to comply with the CDC schedule, he suffers a terrible, terrible, financial punishment from Blue Cross Blue Shield."

What financial punishment is attorney Kennedy talking about?

A recent issue of the Blue Cross Blue Shield handbook, which doctors across America receive, classifies the set of CDC infant vaccines as the combo 10. If pediatricians have 63% of kids in their practice under the age of two fully vaccinated with the combo 10 they receive a bonus. The described bonus is $400 per child.

BCN Commercial HMO payment table

| QUALITY INCENTIVE MEASURES | PLAN GOAL | PAYOUT |
|---|---|---|
| Breast cancer screening | 80% | $100 |
| Childhood immunizations — combo 10 | 63% | $400 |
| Weight assessment and counseling for children: BMI percentile, counseling for nutrition and physical activity | 63% | $150 |
| Comprehensive diabetes care: HbA1c < 8% | 68% | $250 |
| Comprehensive diabetes care: monitoring for nephropathy | 90% | $125 |
| Controlling high blood pressure for hypertension | 75% | $100 |
| Depression management — PHQ9 testing | Flat Fee | $200 |
| Smoking/tobacco cessation counseling | Flat Fee | $30 |

Credit: TTAV Global, LLC

According to the handbook, here's how it works. Let's say a doctor has 100 kids as patients. The plan goal is 63%. If at least 63 of them get vaccinated with the combo 10 before their second birthday, then Blue Cross Blue Shield awards this doctor $400 for *all* 100 children. That equals a financial reward of $40,000 for this doctor on top of his regular income.

By ensuring a certain number of children get fully vaccinated (which means the parent buys *all* the shots) a doctor will receive a bonus payment for having made additional income possible.

How many readers know that pediatricians receive bonus payouts when they inject more vaccines?

Pediatricians make money on both sides when they inject a vaccine – from the parents and from the company as a bonus. Or as a kickback, as they used to say. ==Most people consider this improper or unethical.==

==It's certainly a conflict of interest.== Even if it's legal, it means I can no longer trust that my pediatrician's primary interest is my children. Could this be a reason they urge families to follow the full CDC schedule? As a lawyer, this is what concerns Robert Kennedy Jr.

Pediatricians with a successful practice in large metropolitan areas may have well over 1,000 patients. If at least 630 kids below age two receive the combo 10, Blue Cross Blue Shield rewards these doctors with $400 x 1000 = $400,000.

Now you know why your doctor claims vaccines are safe and effective. That fat inducement income will convince anyone of the benefit of vaccination. American doctors are getting richer at the cost of our kids and grandkids. Do you consider this payout legitimate income for a doctor?

Companies regularly offer inducements to health officials in return for their compliance. The surge in the number of vaccines is stoked by companies shelling out millions of dollars to influence doctors that their product is a safe solution to disease.

## Tobacco Science

Unfortunately, it's not new for doctors, scientists, or celebrities, to promote products for payment. They did it for tobacco companies in the 1950s.

These astonishing Big Tobacco ads from 1953 claim that doctors with "scientific evidence" prove that smoking is harmless!

Credit: promotional ads

Here is the text of one of the ads:

"NOW... Scientific Evidence on Effects of Smoking!

A medical specialist is making a regular bi-monthly examination of a group of people from various walks of life. 45 percent of this group ha**s** smoked Chesterfield for an average of over ten years. After ten months, the medical specialist reports that he observed... no adverse effects of the nose, throat and sinuses of the group from smoking Chesterfield."

Back in the 1950s, tobacco companies hired doctors and celebrities to promote tobacco safety. Such studies are pejoratively known as "tobacco science." Nowadays, everybody knows tobacco can cause lung cancer. A warning label is on every single pack. In these promotions, science was not taking place. Fraud was taking place.

The tobacco companies had their own data, so they knew that tobacco was a carcinogen. But only when we studied and followed millions of people over decades did it become public knowledge.

Who benefited from the "scientific evidence" that smoking cigarettes caused no harm? Only tobacco companies. Millions of people suffered ill effects by trusting doctors who were hired to promote smoking. Finally, tobacco companies were taken to court and had to pay billions in compensation.

Today, pharmaceutical companies use the same strategy. They conduct their own so-called scientific studies to support vaccine safety like the tobacco industry did.

Who benefits when a doctor receives an extra $400 per child for all kids in his practice if only 63% of children under his care receive the combo 10 package before age two? Profit trumps health, and doctors bluff families that childhood vaccines are safe, despite vaccines being legally unavoidably unsafe.

Like tobacco science, vaccine science quotes studies to show that their products are safe. Big money drives the intellectual justification for vaccination treatment. Dubious statistics are dragged from the void and manipulated as propaganda to promote safety and efficacy.

The big difference is Big Pharma lobbied for 100% freedom from liability, so they have avoided the loophole that stopped tobacco companies.

It happened before, and now it's happening again. People need to stand up and demand genuine science. We need to get back to doing genuine studies over decades to scientifically prove that vaccines are safe and effective for the long term.

# ~ 9 ~
# Foregoing Vaccines

> I'm not arguing vaccines are a bad idea,
> I think they're a good thing, but I think
> the parent should have some input.
> The state doesn't own your children.
> Parents own the children and
> it is an issue of freedom.
>
> - Rand Paul, M.D.

Recently, the journal *Pediatrics* published a study showing that educated parents with the highest socio-economic incomes choose to delay or forego the CDC vaccine schedule.

Award-winning science journalist and former Senior Fellow at the Schuster Institute at Brandeis University, Dr. Jennifer Margulis, decided to research whether something was wrong with the CDC schedule or with the parents?

Her research uncovered a well-kept industry secret. Many doctors in America no longer vaccinate their own children according to the CDC schedule. These doctors choose an alternative schedule for their kids based on better health and better science.

Even people working at the CDC don't follow the schedule for their kids. Yet they recommend the full schedule for your kids. How can Dr. Margulis be certain about that?

"I know that because I've talked to them," she asserts. Although she asks doctors who alternate the schedule if she can use their name, they always decline. These are the main reasons; *I don't want to lose my job*. Or, *I'm choosing not to do these vaccines because I know they're not effective.*

"I could never reveal who those people are," because she follows journalistic ethics, "but I can tell you that I have spoken to them myself and they have told me the truth. And the truth is that they are alternating the schedule in their own families for their own children."

If she doesn't maintain confidentiality, her journalism career is over. "I had someone who's an active and very vocal spokesperson for the current vaccine schedule who confided in me. That person did not do the Hepatitis B vaccine, because when that person looked at all of the data that person realized that it wasn't a good idea."

From her research Dr. Margulis concludes, "...we have public health officials screaming from the rooftops that parents must do this vaccine schedule exactly as put out by the CDC, while themselves in their own families they're choosing not to follow it."

What does it mean when doctors promote vaccines they don't trust to use themselves? Sounds to me like they represent the interest of the vaccine industry more than the interest of our children. This is more proof, like the discovery that doctors get bonus payouts for vaccinating more kids.

Are you comfortable with that? If not, you need to find a doctor who has the same ethics as you do. Keep in mind that nobody knows a child better than the mother. Interview doctors until you find one who will work for you. Because you don't work for them.

In a *New York Times* article, "Parents deserve to have a choice about Vaccination" published March 23, 2014, Dr. Margulis wrote:

"There is tremendous evidence showing vaccinations prevent childhood diseases. Should public health officials do everything they can to encourage, inform, and facilitate childhood vaccinations? Yes. Do they have the right to force parents to vaccinate their children? Absolutely not.

"[I]n America we believe parents are capable of making their own decisions about their children's health. We believe in freedom of choice. This freedom of choice extends to when – and even whether – parents vaccinate their kids."

## Science for Sale

The pharmaceutical giants dish out incentives to people in positions of power who "determine" which vaccines are "vital" to public health

Dr. David Lewis has conducted research in microbiology for the EPA. As a senior level research microbiologist, he has worked on everything from climate change to pollutants in the environment. As an insider, he saw how corporations and government agencies funded science and awarded grants to universities for projects intended for promotion in scientific literature. He became concerned about the scientific process within the EPA.

"And I saw the same thing," he revealed publicly, "at the CDC, the FDA, other federal agencies; and the universities that they funded was all geared towards supporting certain government policies and industry practices. Scientists who published data that supported the government's policies and certain industry practices that were economically important became promoted."

On the other hand, if the research generated data "...that raised questions about certain government policies or industry practices, that research would be suppressed. Their research would not be published."

In his book, *Science for Sale*, Dr. Lewis documents his experience working in a system that used public funds in a manner he considered unethical because of a serious conflict of interest.

Credit: http://amazon.com

"The issue of vaccine safety is an issue that I saw firsthand – that certain government agencies and certain universities are manipulating the data in order to protect the sales of vaccines and to cover up any adverse effects."

To cover up adverse effects, they manipulate data? It looks like money really does undermine children's health in the twenty-first century. For readers who had difficulty believing in such manipulation, this book must be an eye-opener.

In the end, Lewis filed several whistleblower lawsuits to enable him to continue his research regardless of the outcome.

The fact is that vaccines are not yet up to the highest levels of safety and efficacy, because most of them are relatively new. It will take at least a decade or two to come to the standard of full safety and protection. Pharma is working on it, but right now they try to sell us that existing vaccines are already at the highest level of safety and efficacy when they're not.

You need to watch the following documentaries by concerned filmmakers who reveal how the vaccination cover-up leads to catastrophe. These are not the positive vaccination films sponsored by the medical industry that you see on TV shows, like Nova and Frontline. These films show the other side of vaccines so you can understand the big picture.

Vaccinating our children:

1. Vaxxed – From Cover-up to Catastrophe –
   A true account of vaccine injured children and the cover-up that ensued – 2016
2. Trace Amounts – Ethyl Mercury – 2015
   https://www.youtube.com/watch?v=pQKglol4OLE
3. Silent Epidemic – the Untold Story of Vaccines - 2013
   https://www.youtube.com/watch?v=lJGyN3gCsBg

4. Vaccine Nation – 2008 –
   https://www.youtube.com/watch?v=j8nrdybZZzA&list=PL057E332958E769C9
5. The Greater Good – Real Stories of Vaccine Injury - 2011
   https://www.youtube.com/watch?v=eU32Ojf8-rA
6. VAXXED Documentary: Explored with Filmmakers
   https://www.youtube.com/watch?v=_KrpK0rbl9w

All military personnel require mandatory vaccination. Vaccinating our military personnel:

7. Direct Order
   https://www.youtube.com/watch?v=wDDMsvErsQw
8. Beyond Treason
   https://www.youtube.com/watch?v=DDQi9uMUodk
9. Lethal Injection
   https://www.youtube.com/watch?v=UhKyWNPJ3q0
10. Killing Our Own
    https://www.youtube.com/watch?v=tFQkgmSaVuk
11. Vaccine Syndrome
    https://vimeo.com/215109690

Perhaps you remember the Gulf War Syndrome epidemic among soldiers returning from the Gulf War. Well, military personnel that did not go overseas also came down with Gulf War Syndrome. All troops were injected with the same vaccines, whether they were stationed overseas or at home. Clearly, the most likely source of the disease was the shots.

How did the vaccine industry become so influential, even over government and military policy? Well, they hire experts who lobby politicians to legislate in their favor in return for inducements, bonuses, and payouts.

Some elected officials no longer represent their constituents because they've been purchased by Big Pharma dollars. This was the case with California Senate Bill 277 which we examine next.

### Real Science Ignored

California Senators Richard Pan and Ben Allen co-authored a bill for mandatory vaccination and the removal of exemptions. The legislation was written and submitted shortly after the Disneyland measles outbreak.

When they presented their bill to the state legislature in June 2015, many people were shocked that such a draconian and cynical statute would surface in liberal California. The media predicted there was no way to stop its passage into law.

To win support, the promo ad shows kids happily dancing and raising their hands for vaccines under a syringe. Does anyone really believe kids think vaccine shots are cool?

Credit: Public Advertisement

It's clear in the photo below that two adults need to restrain an unwilling child as Dr. Charles Goodman vaccinates 12-month young Cameron Fierro with the MMR vaccine on January 29, 2015, in Northridge, California.

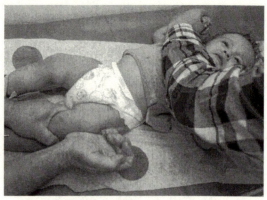

Credit: AP Photo/Damian Dovarganes

Try to find a kid that's not frightened seeing a syringe about to jab them; a stark contrast to pro-vaccine photos of kids happily receiving a shot.

Credit: shutterstock.com

Renowned immunologist Dr. Tetyana Obukhanych sent an open letter to California legislators prior to the vote on SB 277 about the removal of personal vaccine exemptions. She attained her PhD in Immunology at Rockefeller University in New York. She also did postdoctoral work at Harvard Medical

School in Boston and Stanford University in California. She is the author of the book *Vaccine Illusion*.

Credit: amazon.com

The entire letter is reproduced in Chapter Sixteen. For now, I'll only feature the most salient points. Dr. Tetyana begins by stating that she wants to correct common misperceptions about vaccines so that legislators can vote with a fair and balanced understanding supported by accepted vaccine theory and scientific findings.

The first point she addresses is whether unvaccinated children pose a higher threat to the public than vaccinated children. After giving a detailed analysis based on a scientific foundation, she assures legislators that, "a person who is not vaccinated with IPV, DTaP, Hep B, and Hib vaccines due to reasons of conscience, poses no extra danger to the public than a person who is. No discrimination is warranted."

Her second point focuses on how often serious vaccine adverse events happen. After explaining the high level of adverse results, she concludes that, "When the risk of an adverse event requiring an ER visit after well-baby vaccinations is demonstrably so high, vaccination must remain a choice for parents, who may understandably be unwilling to assume this immediate risk in order to protect their children from diseases that are generally considered mild or that their children may never be exposed to."

Her third point examines whether discriminating against families who oppose vaccines for reasons of conscience can prevent future disease outbreaks of communicable viral diseases, such as measles.

After providing statistical evidence Dr. Tetyana states that, "Taken together, these data make it apparent that elimination of vaccine exemptions, currently only utilized by a small percentage of families anyway, will neither solve the problem of disease resurgence nor prevent re-importation and outbreaks of previously eliminated diseases."

Her final point questions whether discrimination against conscientious vaccine objectors is the only practical solution. She answers definitively that it is not a practical solution.

She ends her letter with a summary conclusion of the four points.

"1) due to the properties of modern vaccines, non-vaccinated individuals pose no greater risk of transmission of polio, diphtheria, pertussis, and numerous non-type b *H. influenzae* strains than vaccinated individuals do, non-vaccinated individuals pose virtually no danger of transmission of hepatitis B in a school setting, and tetanus is not transmissible at all;

"2) there is a significantly elevated risk of emergency room visits after childhood vaccination appointments attesting that vaccination is not risk-free;

"3) outbreaks of measles cannot be entirely prevented even if we had nearly perfect vaccination compliance; and

"4) an effective method of preventing measles and other viral diseases in vaccine-ineligible infants and the immunocompromised, immunoglobulin, is available for those who may be exposed to these diseases.

"Taken together, these four facts make it clear that discrimination in a public-school setting against children who are not vaccinated for reasons of conscience is completely unwarranted as the vaccine status of conscientious objectors poses no undue public health risk."

Dr. Tetyana wanted legislators to vote for genuine science from an immunologist citing relevant data and studies. Her letter defeats the false arguments that pharmaceutical companies propagate as scientific.

## Payoff Politics

Despite the overwhelming scientific evidence, in a packed hall of parents Senator Pan was asked to vote on SB 277 or to defer it. Instead of turning to the assembled families who had seen Dr. Tetyana's open letter, he looked over to two men. They came over to speak with him. Then he voted for the bill in front of a packed crowd of parents begging him not to.

Later, the Sacramento Bee newspaper exposed the two men as pharmaceutical lobbyists. Senator Pan received $95,000 from these lobbyists prior to the passage of SB 277. On June 30, 2015, Governor Jerry brown signed this mandatory vaccine bill into law.

There's no record of what Senator Pan received after the vote, or if Senator Allen received money for his vote. But one can reasonably assume that since Allen was a co-sponsor of SB 277, he would expect to get payment for his vote, like Pan.

Nothing good ever comes by accepting funds from companies in exchange for your vote. Essentially, SB 277 removed the right of conscientious objection guaranteed by the U.S. Constitution due to the freedom of religion clause. But that right is being stripped away.

## Foregoing Vaccines

Because many vaccines contain human fetal cells, as well as animal fetal cells, most practicing religious people would be offended by that. Before, they could object to having that chemical concoction injected into their youngsters. But, the constitutional right of religious exemption has now been denied.

Readers who need legal recourse may contact Alan Phillips, J.D., a nationally recognized legal expert on vaccine law. His practice is focused on vaccine waivers, exemptions, and legislative activism. He hosts a weekly online radio show, The Vaccine Agenda.

The Supreme Court has already issued two rulings that religious beliefs do not have to be proven as part of a state-sanctioned/licensed church. Any person or group who tries to force individuals to sign papers that say otherwise, have no constitutional right to do so.

Prior to voting for SB 277, the undeniable science cited by Dr. Tetyana should have been studied by every California legislator. Those who did not take the time to study the science and vote appropriately were guilty of dereliction of duty.

Does anyone think this vote was a case of democratic legislation for and by the people?

It's quite clear something was amiss in the California Senate. They chose to ignore scientific evidence proving there was absolutely no need to deny personal exemptions. The will of the people and the expert testimony of a renowned immunologist played no part in the final vote.

The scandalous passage of SB 277 was tragic because it circumvents the United States Constitution. It was unethical because it ignored scientific evidence, the will of the people, and involved pay-off money.

The California senate allowed fraud to enter the legislative process, and it endangered the lives of innocent children who must be vaccinated or denied a public-school education.

In America, a decree-law is unconstitutional unless there's an emergency. Because no disease epidemic is prevalent, this vaccine mandate is unconstitutional. By removing the right of public-school education and child care benefits for unvaccinated children, it violates the Nuremberg Code signed by the U.S. in 1947 to prevent forced medical interventions.

What is the outcome of this decree-law? A "neglectful" family that refuses to give medical care to their kids can lose custody of their children. Parents in California are nervous about Child Protective Services showing up at their door with policemen to escort their children to "safety."

The kids will become a ward of the state where they can be "protected" with mandated vaccines. In some cases, a parent has been jailed for refusing to vaccinate their youngsters. That's how far government is prepared to go to ensure everybody gets inoculated.

Parents are forced to comply with this new state order enshrined into law by corrupt politicians paid to do so by vaccine manufacturers who benefit by increased profits that will accrue from the upsurge of vaccine sales.

Politicians Pan and Allen are simply puppets of Big Pharma. They have demolished medical choice in California and violated the respected AMA code of medical ethics. They betrayed the people who put them in office by subjugating all children to forced medical intervention.

America was founded on the basis of freedom of religion. Today your religion has no place in California. Families no longer have religious or medical rights to refuse vaccines injected into the body of their child because all exemptions have been prohibited.

Scientific totalitarianism has arrived in California. Democracy was defeated by corrupt politicians taking payoffs for their vote from the pharmaceutical lobby. Gestapo government has replaced freedom of life, liberty, and the pursuit of happiness. This legislation gives us a clue about how life might be like in the next decade.

Due to completely ignoring scientific evidence and the will of the people, this mandatory vaccine law should be repealed and accepted for what it really embodies – criminal corruption.

What was the rationale for ending our freedom to choose vaccines despite the international Nuremberg Code that outlawed forced medicine, co-authored and signed by U.S. government representatives?

Was it simply for corporations to make more money?

Was it for protection against a worldwide epidemic?

Was it really about health, or some hidden agenda?

### Money Equals Control

Nowadays, multinational corporations have more money than most countries. In our world money means monopoly. The more money a company has, the more control they can exert over politicians and policy. They can buy senator's votes and pass laws for their own benefit in any country, including America.

Political corruption leads us to conclude that democracy is being swapped for dictatorship, by greedy corporations that cannot be sued.

The following is the exact wording of the SB 277 legislation:

"...it is the intent of the Legislature to provide a means for the eventual achievement of total immunization of appropriate age groups against the following childhood diseases:
- Diphtheria

## Foregoing Vaccines

- Hepatitis B
- *Haemophilus influenzae* type b (HIB)
- Measles
- Mumps
- Pertussis (whooping cough)
- Poliomyelitis
- Rubella
- Tetanus
- Varicella (chickenpox)
- Any other disease deemed appropriate by the department..."

"Any other disease" leaves the law open to include whatever the state wants to add in future.

"...total immunization" means everybody whether they want it or not.

"...deemed appropriate by the department" means politicians will decide what's best for you, whether you like it or not. That used to be called fascism.

The bill removes all medical exemptions for vegan and vegetarian groups who do not ingest any animal substances which are in most vaccines. All personal belief exemptions based on your religion are gone.

Because the freedom of religion guarantee has been abrogated, as well as the right to choose whatever food one believes is most healthy to eat, this bill turns vaccination into a human rights issue.

Mandatory vaccination also forces parents to pay for shots more, or their children are denied an education. As new children are born every year who will need to be educated, the dollar value of this vaccine legislation skyrockets exponentially. It's a bonanza payout for pharmaceutical corporations.

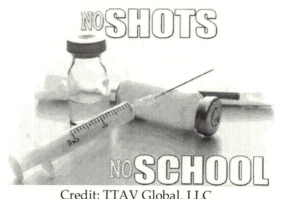
Credit: TTAV Global, LLC

How much money is involved? You can do the math. Again, it's a massive windfall for the vaccine industry.

In European countries, government pays for vaccines as part of national health coverage. But in America this will be expensive for one child. And what to speak of a large family? Underprivileged families will be unable to meet the cost. Do we need more uneducated people in America?

Most doctors are good people trying to help, but they are hamstrung by legislation that forces unwanted injections.

We have a broken system, which discourages questioning medical dogma and encourages physicians to coerce patients into accepting medical procedures they don't want. Can this be healthy for society?

Indeed, the major problem is that this legislation violates the integrity of the US Constitution and the Fourth Amendment of the Bill of Rights, as already clarified in Chapter Five.

Vaccines on Trial

# ~ 10 ~
# Rage Against the Machine

> The greatest threat of childhood diseases lies in the dangerous and ineffectual efforts made to prevent them through mass immunization. There is no convincing scientific evidence that mass inoculations can be credited with eliminating any childhood disease.
>
> - Dr. Robert Mendelsohn, M.D

Many countries follow the lead of the U.S. After all, America is acknowledged as the world leader. Therefore, the Australian government has applied the same draconian measures of forced vaccination.

As of January 1, 2016, the Department of Health has a new vaccination regulation. "Only parents of children (less than 20 years of age) who are fully immunized or are on a recognized catch-up schedule can receive the Child Care Benefit, the Child Care Rebate, and the Family Tax Benefit Part A."

The government slogan in Australia is: No jabs, No benefits.

Only those people who accept the full vaccination schedule are eligible for government benefits and rebates. It really looks like a form of extortion: *you won't get your family benefits and rebates unless you vaccinate your kids.*

Credit: Australian Department of Health

People's individual right to refuse forced medicine has been withdrawn in many countries. What kind of a world are we creating for our children that allows government to forcibly inject medicine into young bodies against the wishes of parents and in defiance of the Nuremberg Agreement signed by all developed nations?

Unfortunately, mandatory vaccination redefines our kids as the property of the state. When the state wields that kind of power it means that democracy is being stripped away from us.

It comes down to valuing money more than valuing lives. Pharmaceutical manufacturers have caused a tragedy by cutting corners and losing public trust. If they weren't so greedy we could have safe vaccines. They have dug this pit with their own dishonesty.

## Tightening the Vice

In Italy, millions have taken to the streets around the country to protest the revoking of individual rights. There have been protest marches in 21 cities across the country. At issue is a proposed mandatory vaccination law for children.

Victor Hugo was right when he wrote, *"No force on Earth can stop an idea whose time has come."*

The Health Minister announced mid-May 2017 that Italy will make vaccinations mandatory for all school children. Unvaccinated kids won't be able to attend state schools. Parents will be required to pay a minimum fine of 500 euros/year and their children may be taken away from such parents, who will be labeled unfit to raise a child.

Due to a nationwide financial crisis, money from Big Pharma alleged to be in the billions per year has corrupted Italian lawmakers. The proposed vaccination law would even allow pharmaceutical representatives to assist in crafting Italian vaccine legislation.

Many citizens say the scheme was hatched in 2014 when the Italian Health Minister Beatrice Lorenzin was chosen to be the world leader for "vaccine strategy." Italy was chosen as the leading country for the WHO worldwide vaccination campaign partially financed by the Bill and Melinda Gates Foundation.

Italians are saying that what happens in Italy will affect many other countries. It's clear there's a strategy to enforce a global vaccination policy for every man, woman, and child. Big Pharma gives financial rewards to elected officials in various countries to legislate against the will of the people.

Gabriele Milani is the father of a vaccine injured child. He warns that doctors who have their pockets lined by vaccine companies today will lose their freedom tomorrow.

**Mr. Milani:** "I am addressing the medical professionals too, who seem to be ignoring that today we are the pioneers of this battle that will concern them eventually. Because they too will lose their freedom of thought. Because they too will not be able to choose what therapies to recommend or advise against. Every one of us is a unique individual, with his unique genetic heritage, so the same drug cannot be mandated to all."

The first opposition march against the new legislation created an influential wave of freedom. Soon city marches began to happen all over Italy. Mainstream news outlets are censoring anti-vaccine information by refusing to report the events and allocate zero airtime to the protests.

But people communicate online via social media. They are determined to continue protesting until the Italian government backs down. When citizens come together for a united cause, it sends a powerful message that can't be ignored.

Due to the people's demands, the government announced revisions to the law although they are still pushing for mandatory vaccination.

Senator Bartolomeo Pepe explains that a Democratic Government should listen to the will of the people.

"What we are fighting for now is not just for vaccines. What is at stake is the freedom of the people, because people are put aside from the interests of multinational corporations such as the pharmaceuticals, like in this case, or oil, or banks. Soon we will have to fight on many fronts."

What's really happening in Italy is a fight to save democracy. These events give us pause to question, if vaccines are so safe and effective, saving millions of lives, why do we need to intimidate people to accept them by force?

If millions of people take to the streets in protest, why does a government legislate against the will of its people? This is not democracy in action. Some people don't want their kids vaccinated. Let it be. Resorting to force under the slogan that it's good for you is suspicious. What's the hidden agenda?

Where are the scientific studies of the vaccinated and unvaccinated over decades to substantiate which group is healthier? There are no studies proving that vaccinating is superior. Pro-vaxxers continue to allege the superiority of vaccination without having studies to back up their claim.

Governmental vaccine policies are tinkering with children's delicate immune systems. Are we playing Russian Roulette with vaccines that are never tested for each child's unique genetic nature? Obviously, different reactions to medication prove that kids are not genetically the same.

How can we predict each child's genetic response to a vaccine, or its side-effects, based on their current health status? We can't. There are no long-term studies to determine who is genetically predisposed to respond negatively to vaccination.

In Italy and the U.S., we see that corporate money can influence government to legislate against its own people. Democracy is finished if corporate finance can override the will of the people.

Now France has announced they will introduce mandatory vaccination in 2018. In Germany, it's also being discussed and could become a reality within a year or two. Big Pharma is systematically paying off elected officials to enact laws in their favor worldwide.

However, in Sweden, cooler heads have prevailed. The Swedish parliament has voted to ban mandatory vaccinations citing 1) "serious health concerns," and 2) violation of citizens' constitutional right to choose their own healthcare.

On May 10, 2017, the Riksdag (parliament) rejected 7 motions intended to enshrine forced vaccination into law. They concluded that, "It would violate our Constitution if we introduced compulsory vaccinations, or mandatory vaccinations."

The decision was based on the Swedish public's "massive resistance to all forms of coercion with regard to vaccinations." The government also referenced "frequent serious adverse reactions" after children were vaccinated.

The following is a condensed English translation of the Swedish report:

"NHF Sweden sent a letter to the Committee and explained that it would violate our Constitution if we introduced compulsory vaccinations, or mandatory vaccinations, as was submitted in Arkelsten's motion. Many others have also submitted correspondence and many citizens have called up Parliament and politicians. Parliamentary politicians have surely noticed that there's a massive resistance to all forms of coercion with regard to vaccinations.

"NHF Sweden also shows how frequent serious adverse reactions according to the rate at which FASS specifies in the package leaflet of the MMR vaccine, when you vaccinate an entire year group. In addition, one must take into account that each age group will receive the MMR vaccine twice, so the side effects are doubled. We must not forget that, in addition, similar adverse reaction lists apply for other vaccines.

"In the letter, we have even included an extensive list of the additives found in vaccines – substances which are not health foods and certainly do not belong in babies or children. We also included for lawmakers a daunting list of studies that demonstrate vaccination is a bad idea."

### Fighting the Corporate Machine

The Swedish decision is a sensible response compared to the U.S. and other countries.

Another serious question: Should government deny an education to children due to mandatory vaccine policy controlled by corporate dollars?

Congressman Bill Posey of Florida thinks that every member of Congress should co-sponsor studies to guarantee the vaccines we give children are safe and effective. He asks why anybody would fear requesting a study.

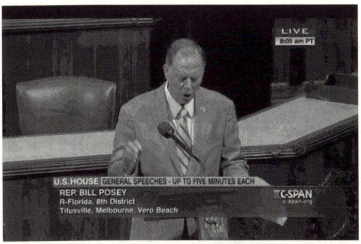
Credit: www.c-span.org

When he raises the issue with his doctor friends they say, *you're nuts. There's dozens of studies.* He replies, *how many of them have you read?* It's because he sees blue-eyed pharmaceutical reps come in with their Super Bowl tickets in hand and talking about dozens of studies that say this and that, but are never shown.

Lobbying is a symptom of corruption in government whereby inducements and payouts are used to influence legislation and votes. The largest meat producers lobby on behalf of animal agriculture and have so much power that they dictate federal policies on food production. Hence, government gives $30 billion to underwrite cheap meat, but zero money goes to vegetable and fruit industries.

Gwen Olsen was a former sales representative in the pharmaceutical industry for more than a decade. Olsen has firsthand experience that an extraordinary

195

number of lethal pharmaceutical drugs are marketed in the U.S. Her book, *Confessions of an Rx Drug Pusher*, is a moving human story of the dramatic turning point in her life when her niece died from a prescription drug she recommended.

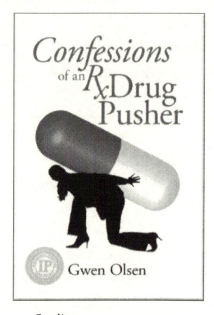

Credit: www.amazon.com

**The Case Thus Far**

Let's sum up the main points of the book so far. When I was a boy only smallpox and polio vaccines existed. Pharmaceutical companies provided vaccines as a civic duty. Marketing vaccines was not a big business.

Then the federal government began ordering hundreds of millions of doses to counteract disease in American children. That's when drug companies realized that vaccines could be a profitable business.

They soon discovered that vaccines were their most profitable product.

Drugs had become increasingly difficult to turn a profit. The biggest problem was testing. New drugs go through long-term safety studies. To do that, they need people who aren't already on some drug. Then they have to place them into a test group. Finding a test group became time-consuming and expensive because almost 1 in 2 persons were on some sort of drug.

Today vaccines are free from liability and have a streamlined process of approval. They don't go through long term safety studies because they're not classified as drugs. Companies don't need to find test groups. So, profit margins increased significantly because many costs disappeared.

Now that the pharmaceutical industry understands that vaccines are the future, they are ramping up production. But for parents, it means the rate of assault on children will be escalating regularly.

The benefits reaped by the vaccine industry are even greater than we first assumed.

## Update

I'm in Italy now and speaking with people. Many were encouraged that Sweden banned all forms of forced vaccinations, but they are outraged that the Italian government approved new vaccination laws in July.

Still, everyone has vowed to continue the fight until the laws are overturned.

The mandatory vaccination decree-law proposed by the Minister of Health was signed by Italian President, Sergio Mattarella. No other decree-law has moved so quickly through the Italian legislative bureaucracy. Previously only 4 vaccines were mandatory, but now that figure triples the number of mandatory vaccines to 12.

The Italian version of the CDC, Instituto Superiore Di Sanità, declared that there was no objective urgency because there are no epidemics in Italy. Factually, cases of measles and meningitis have been substantially lower in the current year compared to the year before.

Local people say that multinational pharmaceutical companies have Italian lawmakers by the jugular. They are not only dictating political policy but are using the corrupt media to silence demonstrations of dissent. News of the recent vaccination law, however, is played up in a positive light on TV.

The Health Minister declared that the new laws will protect the health of our children and all subsequent generations. For minors up to sixteen years of age, vaccines will now be mandatory. Every student up to age sixteen must be vaccinated, or they cannot attend state schools.

The shots will be free of immediate cost as part of the government health care system. That means all vaccine costs will be recouped via increased taxes. The following six vaccines: polio, diphtheria, tetanus, hepatitis B, pertussis, and Haemophilus influenza B (HIB), will be permanently compulsory, and that can never be changed.

These six vaccines will be administered as one multi-dose shot. I don't know about you, but for me that's a lot of chemicals and viruses going into a child's body all at once. No person has ever had these diseases all at once.

A second group of four vaccines: measles, rubella, mumps, and chickenpox will also be administered as one multi-dose shot. Again, a heavy dose of chemicals at the same time.

The government will review these four vaccines at three-year intervals to determine if they remain mandatory according to epidemiological studies and the percentage of children already vaccinated. In other words, they're talking about the so-called herd immunity.

A third group of vaccines (rotavirus, pneumococcal, meningococcal B & C) are strongly recommended but not mandatory, and only in certain regions, but that can be reviewed. Although people will not have to pay for the shots out of pocket, the cost will be reflected in their tax bill.

Unvaccinated kids will not be eligible for kindergarten, and no child care services will be available for any unvaccinated child. This means that the mandatory multi-dose shots are for very young children.

According to the new law, not vaccinating your child will be deemed a violation. Such parents will be summoned to a hearing where they will be levied a fine ranging from 100 to 500 euros and told where and when they must take their child to be vaxxed.

There are limited exemptions: 1) immunity because of having had the disease before, like measles, etc., 2) if doctors sign off that kids are not fit to be vaxxed due to prior clinical conditions, 3) you delay the vaccination for later due to a preexisting condition.

People told me that it was possible to pay money (bribe) at the hearing to avoid the shots. It seems to be all about the money.

There are daily articles in the media ridiculing families who are against vaccination. They are characterized as foolish, superstitious, and against science.

On Sept 16, a large demonstration took place in Venice with over 7,000 people protesting mandatory vaccination. The battle cry of thousands spoke with one voice, FREEDOM.

In every interview mothers, fathers, and grandparents echoed the same mood, *we want to decide.* Italy had a fascist government under Mussolini before and during World War II, so they know what fascism looks and feels like. They do not want to see a return to the past.

When asked why they were against vaccination, lots of people replied, "We are not against vaccination; many of us are favorable, but the Government should nor force us to vaccinate against our free will."

An independent magazine is supporting the people's fight because mainstream media is totally silent. There's no news or comments about the countrywide demonstrations on TV, in magazines, or newspapers. The entire movement is being mobilized online.

The magazine showed photos of demonstrators all over Venice with the following headline: **The Sanitary Inquisition is the New Dictatorship**

The article encourages people not to be afraid but to save lives by civil disobedience. Mandatory vaccination is depicted as a new totalitarian attack on the people. Many people claimed that the decision for mandatory vaccination was taken in Washington three years ago, when Italy's health Minister went to the U.S. in 2014. The new legislation is simply applying that prior decision.

Civil disobedience was the strategy that Mahatma Gandhi used to gain independence for India from the British in the 1940s, and how Martin Luther King achieved civil rights for African Americans in the '60s.

Another huge rally was planned for Rome in late October, after I returned home. In Italy, families are not taking mandatory vaccines lying down. They are taking to the streets to voice their concerns.

## ~ 11 ~
## No Right Of Refusal

> Many here voice a silent view that the Salk and Sabin vaccine, being made of monkey kidney tissue...has been directly responsible for the major increase in leukemia in this country.
>
> - Frederick R. Klenner, M.D., F.C.C.P.

Many countries are increasingly mandating vaccinations for children. Who really benefits from this deluge of vaccines within a child's tender body?

I interviewed a couple whose first child suffered a serious adverse reaction from the MMR vaccine. Now they have a second child on the way and they don't want to take the risk of giving vaccines to their newborn. This is a normal response and follows the proverb, "Once bitten, twice shy."

How would you feel if your first child received a serious vaccine injury? Would you want to give your newborn the same vaccine?

The freedom to choose means we have the right to refuse and not be forced to act against our own judgment and conscience.

Barbara Loe Fisher publicly voices her concern that people are gradually being stripped of their Constitutional rights.

"Individual autonomy, the right to protect bodily integrity, the human right to informed consent to medical risk taking, the human right to follow our conscience, to follow our religious beliefs; these are fundamental rights that define what freedom really means. So, if the government takes that away from us we're no better than slaves. We're no better than people who can be used. We have to have the right to have control over what goes into our bodies and the bodies of our minor children that we are responsible for, legally and morally…We have a moral duty to fight for these rights."

Laura Hayes is a mother of a vaccine-injured child. She became a vaccine activist due to her personal experience of what happened to her child right after getting shots. As a result, she has become a warrior for vaccine choice and clarifies what her nightmare is with vaccine companies:

"Although the 1905 Jacobson decision was erroneous, it still has not been overturned by the 1947 Nuremberg Code, signed by the United States and many other countries that nullified and made void all forced vaccinations. The 2005 UNESCO agreement, which the U.S. also signed, upholds the right of prior voluntary and informed consent prior to any medical intervention, and that includes vaccinations."

The UNESCO Convention of 2005 is another binding international legal agreement that the U.S. signed to uphold as a guarantor. The Convention recognized the Rights of Parties to take measures to protect and promote the diversity of cultural expressions, including religious culture. The Agreement confirmed cultural diversity as a defining characteristic of humanity, which should be cherished and preserved for the benefit of all people.

Therefore, all signatory countries confirmed the right of vaccine choice based on cultural diversity. Mandatory vaccination flies in the face of the UNESCO Agreement, which held that cultural diversity increases "the range of choices and nurtures human capacities and values."

Considering these binding international agreements, the 2011 vaccine legislation in the U.S. contradicts internationally signed legal agreements. Moreover, it has now become even more difficult to get at the truth.

Robert J. Krakow, Esq., is a medical malpractice attorney who represents families with vaccine injured children. He knows that government has assumed the role of supporting the vaccination program, but he's upset to see the pharmaceutical industry collaborate with government to promote a mandatory vaccine agenda.

Under the existing legislation of the vaccine act, government is supposed to publicize the Vaccine Injury Compensation Program and warn citizens about potential risk. He cites a recent report of the GAO (government accountability office) commissioned by Congress, that reveals a profound political policy problem. The people who are pushing vaccines don't publicize the compensation program due to a conflict of interest.

Big Pharma has checkmated parents who are now helpless to protest, while vaccine companies laugh all the way to the bank. One may question what drives people to act in a way that ultimately harms families and children? The simple answer is greed for money, which I define as "lust on steroids."

In the case of U.S. vaccine legislation, it's clear that money remains the root of the evil. Scientists, pharmacists, pediatricians, and office workers connected to Big Pharma will never jeopardize the jobs that support their family, their mortgage, the car payments, college education for their kids, etc. Thus, it goes on, and nobody speaks out against the injustice. These people have all been purchased.

## Choose to Refuse

The example in Italy where people protested forced vaccination has inspired hospital workers in the U.S.

Now more than 22,000 nurses are refusing mandatory vaccines.

Nurses against Mandatory Vaccines (NAMV) began as a response to introducing mandated vaccines in the workplace. The organization is not pro-vaccine or anti-vaccine, but 100% for vaccine choice.

Today, if you work as a nurse and refuse the flu vaccine then you must wear a face mask while on duty. Why are hospitals forcing the issue on their prized nursing staff?

Dr. Karen Sullivan Sibert is a pro-vaccine doctor, yet she opposes this policy. She says that making nurses wear masks for refusing the flu shot violates HIPAA law (Health Insurance Portability and Accountability Act) for patient privacy. Studies now show that flu shots are among the most ineffective of all vaccines. They do not offer any extra protection for hospital patients.

The CDC reluctantly admits that the flu vaccine doesn't always work because of rapid virus mutation. It's almost impossible to make a flu vaccine to match circulating strains of influenza for the season. Moreover, sluggish production means that updated vaccines arrive after the fact.

More significantly, mandatory vaccination forces our nurses, the front line in healthcare, to take a concoction with problematic ingredients. The list of ingredients Sibert cites includes known neuro-toxins such as thimerosal, aluminum, and foreign proteins derived from GMO elements.

Some nurses have chosen to lose their jobs rather than be coerced to take a vaccine they know is unsafe and ineffective. Others are fighting back by suing the hospital, state, and federal governments for refusing to recognize their constitutional rights.

NAMV members believe all people enjoy the undeniable right to choose or refuse medical treatment, and that includes nurses and healthcare workers.

So far, the government doesn't require a total mandatory vaccination policy, but that's rapidly changing. Yet many hospitals take an "all or nothing" stance against healthcare workers who face losing their jobs if they refuse a flu shot. This is not only a human rights violation, but a violation of the international Nuremberg code, as well as violation of the Equal Employment Opportunity Commission (EEOC).

Pro-vaccination advocates state that 30,000 people die from the flu every year. But when you inspect these studies, they lump in pneumonia and other diseases, so they don't reflect true figures for the flu. Because there's no vaccine for pneumonia the skewed figures only muddy the research results.

Factually, most flu strains mutate before an updated vaccine is developed. Looking at published statistics, it's obvious that more people die from heart disease, diabetes, and other health complications, including medical errors.

Hospitals claim that mandatory flu vaccines are for "patient safety." However, *NBC News* reported that the nasal spray flu vaccine, FluMist, was only effective for 3% of patients during the 2015 flu season. How would you like those odds for your contraceptive? In other words, it's mostly ineffective. Still, 30 percent of all the flu vaccines administered to children was the FluMist spray.

NAMV argues that a mandatory flu vaccine policy has never cured the flu. All it does is increase the revenue. The sad consequence is that babies are the most vulnerable victims.

Did you ever ask your pediatrician why he always recommends flu shots for your family? Perhaps you think health insurers and drug companies offer doctors incentives in the interest of public health. But it's always about money because doctors know that flu shots can be ineffective.

So why the big push to force the flu vaccine on people? The Affordable Healthcare Act, also known as Obamacare, established Hospital Value-Based Purchasing. Information online shows that hospital systems must have at least a 90% flu shot reception rate for their staff, or they will lose 2% of their Medicare and Medicaid funding.

This fact gives credence that mandatory flu vaccination policies are not patient-safety driven, but financially driven. The kickback system explains why doctors still push FluMist when they know it rarely works.

There is ample data that suitable hygiene is more effective to prevent the spread of disease than vaccines. The Karachi Health Soap Study in 2002 was a randomized controlled trial performed by Dr. Stephen P. Luby. The goal was to assess the impact of hand washing and bathing with soap in settings where infectious diseases are leading causes of childhood disease and death in Pakistan.

You can view the online study at: http://healthimpactnews.com/2012/study-shows-soap-may-be-more-effective-than-vaccines/

## The War on Values

Where is our country going by mandating vaccines and removing medical and religious exemptions? It looks like the war on disease has become the war on values and beliefs.

There is a concerted effort to marginalize, demonize, and sanction people in this country who don't agree with the one-size-fits-all, no-exceptions, vaccine approach. Government health officials and medical organizations are pushing this view vigorously.

It began with: No shots, No school, and it's now become: No shots, No health insurance. Families won't get health insurance coverage unless they agree with all federal recommended vaccines. No shots, No Medicare or Medicaid.

The NVIC reports that seniors are contacting them and revealing that doctors who have treated them for many years are now saying, "We can't treat you if you don't get the influenza vaccine, the shingles vaccine, and the pneumococcal vaccine."

The NVIC have also received reports from disadvantaged people, poor people on government assistance, who tell the same story.

Reports have come from travelers trying to come to America who won't be able to immigrate unless they get all the vaccines. No shots, No visa.

Barbara Loe Fisher is very concerned with recent vaccine policy.

"I think the public health system is becoming militarized. When you have this marginalization, demonization, of people who want to make vaccine choices, we are facing a future that could be very, very oppressive. Way more oppressive than it is now.

"There are societal sanctions being attached so you won't even be able to get a job, certainly with health care workers. Many health care workers cannot have a job unless they agree to an annual flu shot, and a series of other vaccinations, even if they've got high risk factors.

"There are pregnant health care workers who say, *they want me to get vaccinated but I don't want to get vaxxed while I'm pregnant.* We have had health care workers who had autoimmune disorders, or vaccine reactions. No exceptions – you either get the shots or you're out of a job. There's talk about extending it to child care workers, to teachers, and basically to anyone who works with the public, who performs a service for the public."

By now I'm sure you understand that doctors receive cash rewards for administering vaccines. If you wondered why some doctors refuse patients who choose not to vaccinate their kids, now you know it's another conflict of interest. Again, money trumps health.

NVIC is a health advocate organization. They don't give medical advice, and they don't tell people what to do. Rather, they encourage people to get vaccine information from many sources and make an informed decision.

In case you're wondering, NVIC is not politically aligned with any party. It has always been bipartisan and is funded by private family foundations and individual donations. They began by creating a $3 information packet on the DPT vaccine.

Today their support comes from families with healthy children, families with vaccine-injured children, and from health care professionals. They insist that they never accept money from government agencies or corporations involved with manufacturing vaccines or promoting the use of vaccines.

## One-Size-Fits-All

I realized that if I'm going to write a book that entails criticizing the vaccine system, I had to understand why people running the system were so committed to the one-size-fits-all vaccination approach. So why are they?

Well, the smallpox epidemic put the public health community on the road to eradicating infectious disease by the mass use of vaccinations. They said, "We've done it with the smallpox vaccine, and we're going to do it with the polio vaccine. There are many other infectious diseases out there that we can prevent with the mandatory use of vaccines."

It was an ideological commitment to create better health for everyone. That was the goal. It began as a charitable endeavor. However, nobody stopped to consider whether that was a wise commitment. Nor did anybody confirm whether the one-size-fits-all paradigm might throw more people under the bus than they originally projected.

Barbara Loe Fisher says that committing to a strategy is like taking the hill. We have to ask the question: *how many people are we willing to lose to take the hill?* Pharmaceutical companies have never answered the question of how many people get sacrificed to eradicate disease. Are we talking about 5,000, or

50,000, maybe 500,000, or even 5,000,000 worldwide? They put on the blinders. Ask me no questions and I'll tell you no lies.

However, many parents paid the price because the vaccination risk is 100% for a vaccine-injured child. Everybody has a responsibility, or an obligation, to encourage pharmaceutical companies and government to take a second look at the one-size-fits-all commitment.

Unfortunately, the debate was shut down after 9/11 due to the fear of bioterrorism and weapons of mass destruction. There was widespread fear that terrorists would unleash weaponized microorganisms in America and other countries. So, the federal government created homeland security and other agencies to counter bioterrorism vaccines, and they put a wet blanket on the vaccine risks discussion.

Lately, however, things have gotten worse. Not only has the one-size-fits-all paradigm endured but now there's a demonization of anyone who has another perspective about vaccine safety.

Of all vaccinations the flu shot is most related to the one-size-fits-all commitment. More significant than the flu shots being useless, however, is they can be dangerous.

### Flu Shots

Every quarter, the United States Department of Justice issues a report on vaccine injuries and deaths. For the period May 16, 2015 to August 15, 2015 there were 211 cases of severe adverse reactions and deaths that they acknowledged was due to vaccines.

The Department of Justice report specifically listed 86 of the settlements in their report. They specified the name of the vaccine, the injury, and the amount of time each case was pending before settlement.

Of the 86 settlements, 65 were for injuries and deaths due to the flu shot. The majority of flu shot injuries were for Guillain-Barré Syndrome (GBS). It is unfortunate that our mainstream media doesn't acknowledge vaccine injuries and death settlements from the U.S. vaccine court.

How many people believe that the flu shot actually protects people from influenzas? Not many, and here's the reason. The flu shot vaccine insert openly states that, "there have been no controlled trials adequately demonstrating a decrease in influenza disease after vaccination with FLULAVAL."

In other words, no scientific studies have been done to verify the claim that the flu shot can reduce infection from influenza.

> **FLULAVAL® (Influenza Virus Vaccine)**
> **Suspension for Intramuscular Injection**
> **2013-2014 Formula**
>
> HIGHLIGHTS OF PRESCRIBING INFORMATION
> These highlights do not include all the information needed to use FLULAVAL safely and effectively. See full prescribing information for FLULAVAL.
>
> FLULAVAL (Influenza Virus Vaccine)
> Suspension for Intramuscular Injection
> 2013-2014 Formula
> Initial U.S. Approval: 2006
>
> ----------- INDICATIONS AND USAGE -----------
> • FLULAVAL is a vaccine indicated for active immunization against influenza disease caused by influenza A subtype viruses and type B virus contained in the vaccine. FLULAVAL is approved for use in persons 18 years of age and older. (1)
> • This indication is based on immune response elicited by FLULAVAL and there have been no controlled trials adequately demonstrating a decrease in influenza disease after vaccination with FLULAVAL. (1, 14)

Credit: Flulaval vaccine insert

Doctors and pharmacists who give the flu shots do not hand out the insert sheet with the shot. Now we know the reason. You can request your doctor or pharmacist to give you the insert sheet and point this out to them. You'll need a magnifier because the fine print is so small it's barely readable.

Moreover, when we look closer, the manufacturer admits that, "Safety and effectiveness of FLULAVAL in pediatric patients have not been established." No studies have been done so nobody can say that the vaccine is safe and effective.

> **FLULAVAL® (Influenza Virus Vaccine)**
> **Suspension for Intramuscular Injection**
> **2013-2014 Formula**
>
> **8.3 Nursing Mothers**
> It is not known whether FLULAVAL is excreted in human milk. Because many drugs are ...tion should be exercised when FLULAVAL is administered to a nursing woman.
> **8.4 Pediatric Use**
> Safety and effectiveness of FLULAVAL in pediatric patients have not been established.
> **8.5 Geriatric Use**

Credit: Flulaval vaccine insert

A new study from Ohio State University showed that women who do yearly flu shots have a weaker immune system response in later years. Dr. Lisa Christian is the lead researcher of the study at the Wexner Medical Center, ranked as one of America's best by U.S. News & World Report in 2010.

The study demonstrated that flu shots make people **more vulnerable to influenza infections in subsequent years**. Dr. Christian claims that the study revealed growing evidence, "that those who received a flu shot in the prior year have lower antibody responses in the current year." In other words, flu shots give your body a weakened immune response.

The official narrative of the CDC is that everyone should have a yearly flu shot to ensure protection from influenza infections. Ironically, the Wexner Medical Center study scientifically showed that flu vaccines spread the very infections they are created to negate.

People who took the 2008 flu shots experienced a 250% increase in influenza infections in later years.

But there's even worse news to report on the flu vaccine. No tests have been done to determine if the flu shot affects fertility or is carcinogenic. Why bring up this issue and not test for it? Clearly, the message is, *buyer beware.*

> **13 NONCLINICAL TOXICOLOGY**
> **13.1 Carcinogenesis, Mutagenesis, Impairment of Fertility**
> FLULAVAL has not been evaluated for carcinogenic or mutagenic potential, or for impairment of fertility.

Credit: Flulaval vaccine insert

Science researcher Mike Adams tested Flulaval at his independent science lab in 2014. He wrote that he was shocked to find extremely high levels of toxic mercury. His tests showed mercury levels 25,000 times higher than the maximum allowable EPA level for drinking water. You can read his entire report here:

https://www.naturalnews.com/045418_flu_shots_influenza_vaccines_mercury.html

Other tests conducted via ICP-MS have shown the mercury content in the Glaxo-Kline-Smith flu vaccine at an amazing **51 parts per million**. Again, that's more than 25,000 times higher than the maximum contaminant level set by the EPA for inorganic mercury in drinking water.

According to the vaccine insert sheet Flulaval contains 50 mcg (micrograms) of thimerosal which means about 25 mcg of ethyl mercury for a 0.5 ml dose. Again, if we do the math that's 50 mcg for 1 ml, which comes to 50,000 mcg of mercury per liter.

> **11 DESCRIPTION**
> FLULAVAL, Influenza Virus Vaccine, for intramuscular injection, is a trivalent, split-virion, inactivated influenza virus vaccine prepared from virus propagated in the allantoic cavity of embryonated hens' eggs. Each of the influenza virus strains is produced and purified separately. The virus is inactivated with ultraviolet light treatment followed by formaldehyde treatment, purified by centrifugation, and disrupted with sodium deoxycholate.
> FLULAVAL is a sterile, translucent to whitish opalescent suspension in a phosphate-buffered saline solution that may sediment slightly. The sediment resuspends upon shaking to form a homogeneous suspension. FLULAVAL has been standardized according to USPHS requirements for the 2013-2014 influenza season and is formulated to contain 45 mcg hemagglutinin (HA) per 0.5-mL dose in the recommended ratio of 15 mcg HA of each of the following 3 strains: A/California/7/2009 NYMC X-179A (H1N1), A/Texas/50/2012 NYMC X-223A (H3N2) (an A/Victoria/361/2011-like virus), and B/Massachusetts/2/2012 NYMC BX-51B.
>
> Thimerosal, a mercury derivative, is added as a preservative. Each 0.5-mL dose contains 50 mcg thimerosal (<25 mcg mercury). Each 0.5-mL dose may also contain residual amounts of ovalbumin (≤0.3 mcg), formaldehyde (≤25 mcg), and sodium deoxycholate (≤50 mcg) from the manufacturing process. Antibiotics are not used in the manufacture of this vaccine.
> The vial stoppers are not made with natural rubber latex.

Credit: Flulaval vaccine insert

Whereas for drinking water the EPA allowance is only 2-ppb (parts per billion) of mercury. The mercury in vaccines is alarmingly over the limit allowed for safe drinking water. Moreover, mercury in water or in tuna is orally ingested, so it doesn't have the 100% direct injection potency of a shot.

Does anyone believe it's natural to have mercury directly injected into a child's blood stream? Even if it wasn't 25,000 times higher than what is allowed for eating fish or drinking water, I wouldn't even touch it. Give it to my kids? Never. The flu vaccine is just another gravy train for Big Pharma.

In an interview about the flu shots, Dr. Toni Bark frankly stated, "this vaccine doesn't work. It's a waste of our money; it's a waste of our time."

Dr. Sherri Tenpenny remarked that, "many people who receive the flu shot report getting the flu, shortly after they've gotten the shot. The medical industry says that's virtually impossible."

She explains the science behind influenza. "The flu vaccine is a masterful area of misdirection. Influenza is a disease associated with a group of viruses. At any given time in the United States, there are hundreds and hundreds of strains of influenza. A person who has the flu in various states throughout the country may have completely different strains of flu virus in their system. Every year before flu season, vaccine manufacturers make their best guess about which three strains of influenza virus are we going to put into this year's flu shot. That would be impossible for these three strains to immunize people against the hundreds and hundreds of constantly mutating forms in the wild that influenza disease really involves."

Of course, a business must strive to secure multiple streams of revenue to guarantee their quarterly profit and loss statement is attractive to investors. Businesswise it makes sense, dollars and cents, to persuade government to mandate vaccines so that more products can be sold to more people, even with all the insert disclaimers.

Although mercury and aluminum are toxins that should not be in the human body, when they're together the combination is catastrophic for the mother and her fetus. Yet the CDC recommends both these vaccines for pregnant women: DTaP [aluminum] and flu shot [mercury]. It makes sense for monetary policy or eugenics plans, but not for health.

Unfortunately, most of the American public doesn't seem to understand mandatory vaccination. *I don't have to worry about that now. My kids are past that so I don't have to make a decision.* Others claim they have no say; *my kids have their own kids so they don't listen to me.*

Most people don't see the writing on the wall. For young adults starting a family, the recent legislation in America foreshadows another equally troubling problem.

Democracy is in jeopardy. The deeper meaning is that medical records will no longer remain confidential.

According to researcher Dr. Sherri Tenpenny, losing medical confidentiality is the future for America. It's tied to the use of electronic medical records, which she explains fully in the next chapter.

# ~ 12 ~
# Healthy People 2020

*The further I looked into it the more shocked I became. I found that the whole vaccine business was indeed a gigantic hoax. Most doctors are convinced that they are useful, but if you look at the proper statistics and study the instance of these diseases you will realize that this is not so.*

\- Archie Kalokerinos A.A.M., M.B.B.S., PhD, F.A.P.M.

At the start of this decade, American doctors were advised to install electronic modules for medical billing purposes. This began in 2010, the same year Obamacare was established. The modules were only available from the government at great expense. For example, a Medicare module cost $62,000 and a Medicaid module cost $43,000.

Dr. Sherri Tenpenny explains that many doctors objected to the expenditure. So, the government said, *no problem. We'll pay it for you in exchange for all the medical data.* By 2012 over 500,000 physicians had bought into the system. They were taught how to fill in the electronic records and send the data to the government.

Now, she has released details about a government scheme called Healthy People 2020, which disclosed that adults are also targeted for mandatory vaccination. The National Adult Immunization Plan is a five-year ramped-up system to get every citizen on board.

Most people are unaware that many of the new vaccines in development are focused directly on adolescents and adults. The original adult vaccination guidelines have now become goals for the implementation of Healthy People 2020.

The National Adult Immunization Plan was released in February 2015. The implementation has not been finalized but several ideas are on the table for people not fully vaccinated:

- Will you be able to travel?
- Will you be able to renew your driver's license?
- Will you be able to go to public places for football or basketball games?
- Will you be able to shop at Walmart or Safeway unless fully vaccinated?

Yes, these are the types of things on the table for the near future.

In 2016, a new box for checking appeared on the electronic record: Immunization Status.

This data goes to the Immunization Information System, as well as the Local Regional & District Vaccine Registry. Everyone's information goes into these registries as a cradle-to-grave tracking of their vaccination status. Goodbye confidential medical records.

Dr. Tenpenny explains that the plan for adult vaccination, "actually has language in it that says they want adults to demand and request their vaccines. If they haven't demanded and requested them then they will be offered to them."

She reports that even most doctors don't know 140 vaccines are in the developmental pipeline. Eventually every single person will be required to have every vaccine currently on the market, and every vaccine coming in the future. Doctors will be offered financial incentives to administer adult vaccines, similar to the payouts they now receive for child vaccinations.

The Healthy People 2020 initiative began in 1990 when the Surgeon General and the Department of Health created Healthy People Guidelines. The aim was to look at the overall health of our society, like smoking, obesity, clean water, wearing motorcycle helmets, etc. This resulted in setting up laudable goals to achieve from 1990 to 2000.

Every decade they established new goals. In 2010 they created goals to be achieved by 2020. In 1990 there were 15 original goals and almost 225 objectives. Today the 2020 guidelines have 44 goals and 1,200 objectives that look at every corner of our health, every corner of our life.

Healthy People 2020 is trying to get everybody on board and vaccinated by the end of the decade. The goal is to have at least 90% of the population vaccinated with all available shots. Initially these were set up as guidelines but are now goals. One of the steps is to take away your right to refuse, like what happened with California SB 277.

According to the U.S. Constitution and the Nuremberg Code, no government has the right to force citizens to inject multiple types of chemicals into their children. The Healthy People 2020 project is an insidious and violent attack on humanity because it eliminates the right of refusal.

## The Decade of Vaccines

When the new guidelines for Healthy People 2020 began in 2010, Bill Gates declared in January that this is the year of vaccines. His private agenda, however, was that this would be the decade of vaccines.

As a start to fund activities to "help poorer countries" the Gates Foundation invested $10 million in Liquidia Technologies, a biotech company developing vaccines. This was the initial program in January 2010 to make the next ten years the decade of vaccines.

How much money is involved if every person on Earth has to pay for vaccinations? If you don't want to do the math, it's in the billions of dollars every year, just in America alone. When we consider the entire world, the annual figure is astronomical. That amount of money can influence a lot of decisions, a lot of ethics, and a lot of legislation.

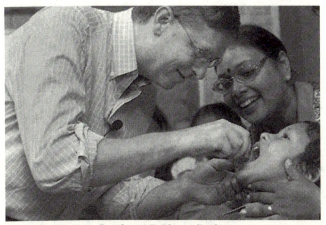

Credit: AP Photo/India

One may wonder why the world's richest man administers the oral polio vaccine containing the live virus to children in India. Well of course, he has invested in the vaccine business via Liquidia Technologies. Gates has publicly stated that he loves vaccines. But does he mean for his own family too, or just for everybody else?

The Gates Foundation is also funding the introduction of GMO seeds into Africa under the Alliance for a Green Revolution in Africa. The show is fronted by Kofi Annan, the former Secretary-General of the United Nations. Because he's a renowned African leader, the expectation is that the African people will accept his judgment that the program is beneficial.

Credit: Alliance logo

In line with the Healthy People initiative for the present "decade of vaccines," the U.S. government has made it necessary to:

- have electronic medical records and tracking
- take away people's right to refuse vaccines
- ramp up the 2020 guidelines and turn them into goals

This venture now includes every person worldwide. How do we know? Because the Gates Foundation has funded a project called GAVI (Global Alliance for Vaccination and Immunization). In 2000 they originally funded the project with a donation of $750 million. Since 2001, the Gates foundation has invested $6.8 billion dollars in this project to vaccinate the world.

Now at the end of 2017, the Healthy People 2020 initiative is well on its way. Within the three years until the end of 2020, citizens of the world must become aware that their rights and freedoms are being stripped away.

Once again, people need to understand who benefits from this worldwide vaccination program and who suffers as a consequence. If people's freedom is slowly being stripped away, then it's clear that the general public is being duped because we are paying for vaccine programs that steadily reduce our liberty and our civil rights.

A tremendous amount of information has come to light over the past few years due to the internet. This has taken the vaccination issue out of the realm of 'conspiracy theory' and into the realm of serious inquiry.

Legislation efforts across the country continue to increase. The government is setting requirements for mandating and tracking vaccines, as well as limiting exemptions.

### Return to Eugenics

Vaccines that have sterilized mice in lab experiments are now the same vaccines administered to people in third world countries. Does that look like the resurrection of a eugenics program to you?

Using the Ted Talks format in February 2010, Bill Gates presented his view for the future. He explained that the world population was 6.8 billion people and was heading up to about 9 billion.

"Now if we do a really great job on new vaccines healthcare, and reproductive health services," he said, "we could lower that by perhaps ten to fifteen percent." Vaccines healthcare means vaccinations; reproductive health services means abortions.

For many people, vaccines represent saving lives. But for Gates, vaccines healthcare and reproductive health services means reducing fifteen percent of the world population. As of the end of November, 2017, the world population is 7.58 billion. Reducing this figure by 15% brings the world population to 6.443 billion after vaccination and abortion.

Let's have a look at the GAVI website: http://www.gavi.org/about/mission

This is the GAVI mission statement: "Saving children's lives and protecting people's health by increasing equitable use of vaccines in lower-income countries."

What does this really mean? The "lower-income countries" are the poor countries that will be inundated with increasing use of vaccines. These countries will also receive the GMO seeds from the Alliance for a Green Revolution in Africa.

There seems to be a huge disconnect between saving children's lives and protecting people's health with reducing the world population by 15%. Saving lives and protecting health sounds like increasing world population. The language hides the intent. You can connect the dots...

Of course, Healthy People 2020 has become a worldwide program, so the same population reduction scheme is also at work in affluent countries.

## Regulating the Vaccine Industry

As an environmental attorney, Robert F. Kennedy, Jr., has been investigating the vaccine industry, as well as government officials who are supposed to regulate the vaccine industry in the interest of public safety. He says that scrutiny of the pharmaceutical industry and the government regulators is not being authorized.

"Rather the opposite has happened, resulting in incentivizing the worst kind of behavior by both Big Pharma and the regulators who have become like a captive agency phenomenon. CDC is really part of the vaccine industry, almost like a subsidiary of the vaccine industry, and that's not hyperbole because CDC buys and sells over $4 billion of vaccines annually!

"If demand for those vaccines are reduced, there are severe economic consequences for the agency. So they sell those vaccines and they create demand for them. Moreover, CDC and FDA are partners in owning vaccine patents. Plus, the Advisory Committee of Immunization Practices (ACIP), which controls the vaccine program, is mainly composed of people who have direct financial ties to the vaccine industry, or vaccine industry insiders, because there are huge financial incentives to add a vaccine to the schedule."

The situation in California and New York has turned into a vaccine frenzy. Now children can't go to school without being vaccinated. Families feel manipulated to pay for vaccinations, or their kids are denied an education.

Low income families, who don't have the money to adequately feed their children, are on food stamps so their kids can eat. But a new policy says they will have to vaccinate their kids to continue on food stamps.

Families are forced to vaccinate because they're afraid the state will take away children from "neglectful" parents who don't protect their kids from disease.

How many readers know that a child can be taken from a family who chooses not to vaccinate? It's a disgrace that in the U.S. children can be taken from parents who feel vaccination could harm their child, or if it's against their religion, or for what they believe is best for their child. Is America still the land of the free and home of the brave?

In West Virginia, California, and Mississippi there is no religious exemption, only a medical exemption. Under certain state laws, the fact that your first child had an adverse reaction is not a good enough reason to avoid vaccinating your second child.

If a child has a genetic predisposition and could be harmed by vaccination, that is now an insufficient reason for exemption under certain state laws. Your child must first take the shot and be injured before you can get a medical exemption. In Texas, Florida, even New Jersey, it's easy to opt out, but nobody can opt out in New York or California.

In America, vaccines are legally "unavoidably unsafe." It means they come with a risk, and there's a table of injuries listed in the VAERS compensation program. From 2003-2015 VAERS recorded 127 measles vaccine related deaths (MMR), while in the same period there were only two deaths from the measles disease itself. This report came from the WV Senate Education Committee.

Clearly, the measles vaccine has caused more harm to children than the measles disease. Yet, you do not have a choice to refuse a forced medical procedure, which mandatory vaccination certainly is.

How have the courts allowed such a criminal undertaking to take place in the land of the free? Well folks, your right to refuse is overridden by the 1905 Jacobsen case. Yes, that was more than a hundred years ago, was during an epidemic, and a person could opt out with a $5 fine.

Obviously the 1905 court would have no idea about the tremendous socioeconomic advances made over more than a hundred years, nor what kids are faced with in 2017. Nonetheless, that 100-year-old law is still on the books and is being applied to every child in America, except for the $5 opt-out fine.

Mothers and fathers must stand up and fight to protect their rights as parents, to protect the rights of their children, and to protect other parents in the same situation, who are forced to vaccinate their kids because there will be consequences in terms of losing services for their children.

In New York, every kid has to have a yearly flu shot, plus a slew of vaccines by age fourteen in order to go to school. A blanket Medical Exemption is nearly impossible. The only hope is a religious exemption, but that bumps up against 1905 Jacobsen. How can that still stand in twenty-first century America?

Mandating vaccines violates due process. Most people don't know that because they're not trained in law, but that's the problem today. Why should an individual be forced to take a vaccine when they have a right of due process to refuse?

Congress has recognized that vaccines do cause harm, and the $3.56 billion in payouts from VAERS supports that, yet some state governments, like New York and California, do not recognize it. They mandate individuals to take shots, and that violates their right of due process.

Physicians understand that a medical procedure can never be forced on anyone. Each person has a right to decide if they want to take that risk. If something goes wrong, they can't blame anyone because it was their choice.

Pharmaceutical companies, however, are bullies that terrorize individuals to take what they don't want. They use lobbyists, and doctors who profit from vaccines, to prevent people from exercising their right of refusal.

Because of the Internet and social media, it's no longer one voice alone in the courtroom. There are hundreds of thousands of voices of educated mothers and fathers who are angry that Pharma has messed with their precious cubs.

These are well-informed women, not quacks, who are organized and understand their Constitutional rights. They are very serious because their kids are getting sick from the shots, and they know they have a right to refuse. The most formidable opponent is an angry mother trying to protect her child.

In Roe v Wade, 1973, the Supreme Court recognized an individual's right to accept or refuse medical treatment, regarding abortion. Vaccination is also medical treatment, so this is no different.

The U.S. sets a standard for human rights around the world. However, in the American homeland there's no longer any guarantee that you're going to enjoy your rights without restrictions. People's rights are being burdened practically every day all over the country.

Our Constitution guarantees justice and redress for all, but it's being denied. The courts will have to balance the vaccine issue because more and more people have a belief that's contrary to vaccination.

In civilized countries, nobody does experiments with children. Every child has a due process right to refuse an injection when the doctor pulls out the syringe. The courts have to decide whether public health is being served sufficiently by vaccines in order to mandate individuals to accept an intervention that may harm them. That is the due process issue. Vaccination is absolutely a human rights issue.

Congress has recognized that vaccines are not safe and that's why we have had the VAERS reimbursement program for kids who've been injured since 1986. It's a fact that the Supreme Court has ruled that vaccines are unavoidably unsafe, so legally we know the shots are unsafe.

Even more horrifying is the manipulation of disease. How many readers know that many vaccines now come from China? Who knows who's transporting them, and if they are appropriately refrigerated? Tainted substances like bovine and pig cells have been found in vaccines. Such ingredients defile the blood and are toxic to the immune system, yet we inject them into a newborn baby? It's beyond ridiculous.

Certain vaccines come from unidentified secret labs in Eastern Europe. We don't know the ingredients, and we're not even sure where they come from. I'm not giving my baby some shot from a secret lab. It's crazy. Such behavior shouldn't be tolerated in the U.S.A.

Many people are afraid because Big Pharma marketing is based on creating fear. Even worse, it's a profit driven industry with lobbying in government, payouts to politicians and doctors. It is disgusting to decent people.

In America today, the moment a child is born, the infant receives a hepatitis shot, even sometimes without the mother being told. Why would anyone want to inject a perfectly healthy baby with hepatitis, or any other shot, on the first day of life?

Intelligent readers also know that nearly every official source speaks dishonestly to the public. All "official sources" on vaccines, for example, are untruthful about vaccine composition and vaccine safety. All "official sources" on agricultural chemicals, like glyphosate, are constantly deceitful about the risks of toxic chemical exposure.

Religious exemption is a parent's choice to live their own life for the family. They deserve it. These parents don't deserve to have people turn their backs on them because of their choice of how they want to care for their family.

It's our choice. And it should be respected, but it's not. It's ignored by politicians who are neglecting the rights of citizens.

Everybody needs to get involved to prevent the breach of our Constitutional freedom. Unless a change comes, and comes soon, "a hard rain is gonna fall" on an unsuspecting public.

Three major changes are required:
- Ban Mandatory Vaccination
- Restore Parental Right of Informed Consent
- Repeal the 1986 Health Act

State authorities need to respect the fact that our family doctor who we trust, gives an opinion, and this is the only person I will trust with my daughter's health. Conventional medicine doesn't work for our family. Our choices as parents should be respected.

History teaches that when choice wasn't respected in other countries, people left and came to America where they were guaranteed freedom of choice. But now this is changing in a negative way. People will again choose to leave America and go to another country that respects a family's freedom.

Dr. Tenpenny reveals to citizens that, "There are 63 chemicals contained in vaccines and 4 of them are documented carcinogens that are being injected at very early ages in children. We are damaging DNA, with chemicals, pesticides, dioxin, and genetically modified food. Once you damage and destroy the DNA, we don't know how many generations that's going to pass down to.

"If we continue with more and more vaccines, and there are at least more than 20 in the pipeline right now, headed for adolescents and adults. They're not stopping in their manufacturing process, so the road that we're on right now with more vaccines, more genetically modified food, all of these horrible pesticides, the prognosis for our collective grandchildren on the road we're currently on isn't good. It simply isn't good."

Where does it stop? It stops by all of us just waking up, and saying *what's going on here and how do we stop this?*

Who can force anyone when it comes to their own body? It's a disgrace.

The toxic ingredients in vaccines, the preservatives like formaldehyde, mercury, and the aborted fetal cells are shocking. The unnatural substances like the monkey, bovine and pig tissue would seriously outrage a lot of people from various religions, not just mine.

It's terrible that parents don't know what ingredients are being injected into the blood stream via vaccination. If you know about these ingredients and it's ok for you, fine, but many people don't want these things injected into their bodies. Why are we being forced against our own choice and better judgment?

Vaccines on Trial

# ~ 13 ~
# The Big Pharma Lobby

> Vaccination is a barbarous practice and one of the most fatal
> of all the delusions current in our time. Conscientious
> objectors to vaccination should stand alone,
> if need be, against the whole world,
> in defense of their conviction.
>
> Mahatma Gandhi

For the last two decades, state medical boards have liberalized the laws governing opioid prescriptions for treating chronic non-cancer pain. This resulted in dramatic increases in opioid use. Many groups supported the use of opioids in large doses due to increased awareness of the right to pain relief.

The present opioid epidemic erupted because of changes in the laws governing opioid prescription. The Joint Commission on the Accreditation of Healthcare Organizations (JCAHO) introduced new pain management standards in 2000 due to aggressive marketing and lobbying efforts by Big Pharma.

Increased opioid use, based on unreliable science and misinformation, is accompanied by a dangerous idea that opioids are extremely safe and effective when prescribed by physicians. On the other hand, there's a mountain of side-effects that comes printed in each prescription packet.

**The Pharmaceutical Lobby**

Two middle-of-the-road newspapers, *The Guardian* and *The Washington Post*, have written critical exposes on the brazen pushing of the opioid epidemic by pharmaceutical companies.

*The Guardian* documented that, "drug makers have poured close to $2.5 billion into lobbying and funding members of Congress over the past decade." Yes, Big Pharma has spent more money wooing politicians than has any other industry.

"Nine out of ten members of the House of Representatives and all but three of the U.S.'s 100 senators have taken campaign contributions from pharmaceutical companies seeking to affect legislation on everything from the cost of drugs to how new medicines are approved."

Pharmaceutical companies in the U.S. charge higher prices for their drugs than is charged for comparable medications in Canada and European countries. They not only push dangerous opioids on anyone who will take them, but they shamelessly pay kickbacks to healthcare providers who write as many opioid scripts as possible. The Surgeon General had to reprimand doctors across the U.S. for promoting Pharma at patients' expense.

In 2016, the pharmaceutical industry spent over $152 million on shaping legislation to control laws and policies that will bolster its profit margins. For every member of Congress, there are almost two pharmaceutical lobbyists to ensure that dollars will continue flowing into Big Pharma coffers.

*The Washington Post* wrote that pharmaceutical lobbyists influenced several members of Congress to successfully get the Justice Department and Drug Enforcement Agency (DEA) to agree to a more "industry-friendly" law. Unfortunately, the new law undermined the DEA's efforts to stop the flow of pain pills to the black market. It also made it virtually impossible for the DEA to clamp down on suspicious narcotics shipments. Big Pharma poured over $102 million into this effort between 2014 and 2016.

Joseph T. Rannazzisi handled the DEA division responsible for regulating the drug industry until 2015. He admitted that, "The drug industry, the manufacturers, wholesalers, distributors and chain drugstores, have an influence over Congress that has never been seen before. I mean, to get Congress to pass a bill to protect their interests in the height of an opioid epidemic just shows me how much influence they have."

The level of corruption and control over U.S. lawmakers by the pharmaceutical companies has reached such proportions that even the media can no longer tolerate it. They have exposed that addictive drugs, including opioids, claim over 64,000 lives a year in the United States.

On October 28, 2017, Mike Adams reported that a pharmaceutical company owner was arrested for running a criminal drug cartel. Here is the report of the Insys Therapeutics raid according to the Daily Caller News Foundation.

"The Department of Justice (DOJ) charged John Kapoor, 74, and seven other current and former executives at the pharmaceutical company with racketeering for a leading a national conspiracy through bribery and fraud to coerce the illegal distribution of the company's fentanyl spray, which is intended for use as a pain killer by cancer patients."

The *New York Post reported* that the company's stock price fell more than 20 percent following the arrests.

"Kapoor stepped down as the company's CEO in January amid ongoing federal probes into their Subsys product, a pain-relieving spray that contains fentanyl, a highly-addictive synthetic opioid. Fentanyl is more than 50 times stronger than morphine, and ingesting just two milligrams is enough to cause an adult to fatally overdose.

"The series of arrests came just hours after President Trump officially declared the country's opioid epidemic a national emergency. Drug overdoses led to 64,070 deaths in 2016, which is more than the amount of American lives lost in the entire Vietnam War.

"As the opioid crisis has developed, more and more states have begun holding doctors and opioid manufacturers accountable for over-prescribing and over-producing the highly-addictive painkillers.

Attorney General Jeff Sessions declared in a prepared statement:

"More than 20,000 Americans died of synthetic opioid overdoses last year, and millions are addicted to opioids. And yet some medical professionals would rather take advantage of the addicts than try to help them.

"This Justice Department will not tolerate this. We will hold accountable anyone – from street dealers to corporate executives — who illegally contributes to this nationwide epidemic. And under the leadership of President Trump, we are fully committed to defeating this threat to the American people."

It looks like the fight is on to end drug cartels and health care monopolies that are crippling America. What to speak of Big Pharma vaccines, the autism cover-up, and the corruption at the CDC. Soon the vaccine fraud and medical corruption scandal will be exposed and we may see many pharmaceutical officials arrested.

# ~ 14 ~

# What's in Those Vaccines?

*The vaccine is a filthy substance and it is foolish to expect that one kind of filth can be removed by another.*

- Mahatma Gandhi

Labels are mostly used to disassociate a poor medical prognosis from the vaccine injury spectrum. Doctors want to put labels on medical conditions. They will talk about immune and brain dysfunction which is part of the vaccine injury spectrum. But that's exactly what autism is – immune and brain dysfunction.

Instead of calling it immune and brain dysfunction they substitute the autism label so it's not part of the vaccine injury spectrum, which means not caused by vaccines. But brain damage by any other name is still brain damage.

Another example. The DPT vaccine was associated with infantile spasms (also known as the jackknife seizure). It had a catastrophic prognosis and most children became severely mentally retarded. It was a seizure disorder but was given a different label – infantile spasms. It doesn't matter how they spin it. The truth is the truth.

Please visit www.CDC.gov or go to Chapter Seventeen where I have posted the CDC vaccine excipient schedule. You need to look for **WI-38** and **MR5** cells. These cells come from human aborted fetal tissue, but there's non-human DNA cells in vaccines too.

We already introduced Dr. Paul Thomas as a board-certified pediatrician for over 30 years, founder of Physicians for Informed Consent, and a member of the Academy of Pediatrics.

He is upset that most of his peers are unaware that aluminum is in the vaccines they administer to children. Doctors are not well versed about the vaccines they prescribe, yet they recommend them for your kids.

When Thomas was in med school, doctors were taught that aluminum is safe to inject into a baby's body. But today, who wants aluminum injected into their baby? Even if it's just a trace amount?

Dr. Suzanne Humphries explains that vaccines are classified as either 1) live or, 2) dead. Live vaccines simulate the disease in the immune system more successfully than dead vaccines; they influence the immune system better. It's the dead, or killed, vaccines to which they add the aluminum adjuvant.

## What's in Those Vaccines?

According to Dr. Humphries although vaccines may give kids a "super-charged immune system" for a brief time, it's not a natural state for the immune system. Moreover, it's not a healthy state for the immune system over the long term.

She clarifies that this temporary super-charging of the immune system does not promote long-term health. The aluminum adjuvant triggers an allergic response in most people. These dead-type vaccines do not strengthen the immune system to fight other infections; instead you become more susceptible to other diseases.

Humphries cites research in Denmark. The study examined hospitalization rates for various infections in children below age four who were injected with either live or dead vaccines. The study showed that when a dead vaccine was the last shot, it had a detrimental effect on the child's overall immune reaction to other infections.

Researchers agree that vaccines contain excitotoxins that can disrupt a child's immune system. Also, it can damage developing brain structures thus raising the risk for a wide range of diseases, learning disabilities, and psychiatric disorders. New studies have provided evidence for a link between the high number of vaccines and the autism epidemic.

Moreover, aluminum research has shown adverse effects on a child's natural immune defense system which helps explain the increase in autoimmune diseases.

## Thimerosal

Besides aluminum, ethyl mercury is also an ingredient in many vaccines but only as a trace amount so it doesn't need to be listed. The mercury-based preservative thimerosal plays no role in making vaccines effective because it's a preservative and only provides a longer shelf life.

Long shelf life prevents loss of sales due to a product going off. Although public pressure has forced the CDC to remove thimerosal from vaccines, it's still there as a "trace amount" and continues to be administered to children and pregnant women via the flu vaccine.

We need to understand mercury toxicity and its exposure in vaccines. The mercury in thimerosal is the chief danger, particularly for our most vulnerable youngsters. People who claim that science has exonerated mercury from any link to autism haven't read the scientific studies.

When you ask a person, *which study are you referring to?* no one can name a study they have read. It's alarming that people can be so vocal, yet ignorant about genuine science. Factually, there are hundreds of studies showing how thimerosal is destructive to brain tissue in both humans and animals.

Furthermore, many studies have linked mercury to autism. Anyone can access these studies on PubMed.

There's a tremendous gap between the government's characterization of the science, which sways public perception of the mercury/autism issue, and what the actual scientific studies have shown.

## Vaccine Inserts

Always read the vaccine insert before agreeing to vaccinate. Whatever you don't understand ask your pediatrician to explain. Most doctors continue to refill prescriptions year after year and they never read the insert listing ingredients and side-effects. That's why they don't understand the long-term consequences of relying on drugs and vaccines for protection.

Building a healthy immune system with nourishing food and exercise is much cheaper and more effective than any drug or vaccine you can take. Remember, medicine is taken when one is ill, but vaccination is given to those who are in good health.

Who reads the flu vaccine and DTaP inserts for pregnant women? They both contain aluminum and mercury (thimerosal) which in combination are very destructive to the human body.

Many vaccine ingredients include: animal DNA, human DNA, viruses, detergents, preservatives, adjuvants, formaldehyde, polysorbate 80, aluminum, mercury, borax, fetal cells. These are injected into our children to protect them from disease?

Social anthropologists in 2068 are going to look back at today's vaccine situation, plus the tobacco hoax of the '50s, and recognize it was all about commerce. Dr. Tenpenny believes we are only one generation away from corrupting the human DNA to the point of no return. She says we'll be so pharmaceuticalized, that there will be little hope of returning to normal.

The vision-statement of the pharmaceutical companies is that every human on earth will be on a minimum of 2 pharmaceutical drugs per day for life. What better way to implement that than to start with newborns on their first day of life (or even *in utero*) to crush their immune systems and make them completely dependent on drugs and vaccines. This is how to make them become customers for life. It's the business model for lifetime customers starting on day one.

What other conclusion can anyone arrive at with two shots on the first day of life now being implemented in America?

When will parents become more fearful of what's coming through a hypodermic needle than about a bacterial or viral infection that will come and go in a week? Plus, childhood illnesses leave kids with lifelong immunity from that particular infection into the bargain.

Pharmaceutical companies prey upon the psyche of parents with tales of how people, and especially children, died from disease until vaccination saved the human race. Today, nobody knows if your child will live through measles, mumps, or chicken pox. That's a huge disconnect between perception and reality. They have rewritten the history.

To protect infants from disease, the best treatment is mother's breast milk, good hygiene, and nutritious food. Dr. Christian Northrup agrees. "Thinking that baby formula is as good as breast milk is believing that thirty years of technology is superior to three million years of nature's evolution."

### Big Pharma influence

Robert F. Kennedy Jr. has been researching the vaccine issue for years. He claims that scrutiny of the pharmaceutical industry by government officials, who are charged to regulate vaccines for the public safety, has been lax, at best. At worst, government regulatory agencies have been captured by the pharmaceutical lobby, which doles out millions of dollars for votes and legislation, as we've already learned.

The CDC has become almost like a subsidiary of the vaccine industry. They own patents on many vaccines that they sell for over $4 billion annually! If demand for those vaccines is reduced, there are severe economic consequences for the agency. So they create demand for their vaccines and sell them to their departments around the country.

Furthermore, Kennedy reveals that the CDC and FDA are partners in the vaccine patent business. The

Advisory Committee of Immunization Practices (ACIP), which controls the government vaccine program, is composed of people with direct financial ties to pharmaceutical industry insiders, because there are huge financial incentives to add a vaccine to the CDC schedule.

Consider the case of Dr. Paul Offit. He's a vaccine industry spokesperson, an insider, who's on the payroll of Merck (the biggest U.S. vaccine producer). In 1999, Offit sat on the ACIP and voted to put the rotavirus vaccine on the schedule. At the same time, he was patenting his own rotavirus vaccine, yet he did not recuse himself.

Offit invented a vaccine (RotaTeq) that contains two strains of a deadly pig virus called circovirus — a virus responsible for killing millions of piglets in China. Circovirus has absolutely nothing to do with helping children fight off Rotavirus, which is a rather mild flu-like infection that causes diarrhea.

Here's a quote directly from Merck's Rotateq printed vaccine product, on page three, last paragraph:

*Parts of porcine circovirus (a virus that infects pigs) types 1 and 2 have been found in RotaTeq.*

Once rotavirus was on the CDC schedule, it created an opening for Offit's vaccine which became enormously profitable for him as a direct result of his vote. Later, he sold that patent for multimillions. Clearly, a huge

## What's in Those Vaccines?

conflict of interest. Of course, as a public servant his duty was to oversee vaccine safety for children.

Naturally, Offit's transaction caused a scandal at HHS. The Inspector General of HHS investigated that practice. His final ruling declared that Offit's transaction was bad, but not illegal under CDC rules. In other words, by adjusting the rules you get away with murder, via the rules. But doesn't anybody care about the children?

In his investigation, Kennedy claims that 64% of the people who sit on that ACIP advisory committee may have the same kind of financial entanglement conflict as Offit. Even more disturbing is that almost 97% of the committee members either had a conflict of interest in the past, or failed to fill out the legal disclosure papers indicating whether they had a conflict or not.

Could Offit's RotaTeq vaccine be the cause of the massive U.S. outbreak of circovirus, also known as PV-777, or PEDV (porcine epidemic diarrhea virus)? Since Rotavirus causes diarrhea in children, who would ever suspect that the RotaTeq vaccine is the actual cause?

Of course, Paul Offit covers all this up with propaganda online. In January of 2012, America's pork industry was devastated by a massive outbreak of porcine diarrhea. The medical industry claims the disease is not transferable to humans, but what about when you inject two strains of it into muscle tissue through a syringe?

Nearly all piglets that get the disease die of it, so what about children injected with it? Could this be why America is experiencing a massive spike in autism, and why the vaccine court has paid out $3.56 billion in compensation to vaccine-injured families?

Dr. Paul Offit is a dominating moderator on Wikipedia and describes himself as a pharma shill (which means he's on pharma's payroll). He says it's safe to eat MSG and high fructose corn syrup (HFCS), and that health nuts are going overboard worrying about them. He promotes Monsanto's deadly DDT pesticide, leaving a trail of nonsense strewn across the internet.

## U.S. Vaccination Law

It's hard for many to believe that the exponential increase in the number of shots given to children is simply based on public health, when people who sit on the decision-making committee are personally profiting from these transactions.

To sum up, here's how the system works today in America. The federal government indemnifies pharmaceutical manufacturers from liability. Committee members making policy decisions about putting vaccines on the schedule have a conflict of interest. Then a government agency, the CDC, holds vaccine patents and distributes these vaccines to reap big money. It's troubling because profit is eclipsing our children's health.

Attorney Kennedy attributes the 1986 Health Act for changing the vaccine schedule. Due to the blanket immunity from all liability, the schedule began to drastically change in 1989 (the legislation became effective in 1987). No matter how reckless Big Pharma behaves, no matter the ingredients, no matter how egregious the injury to the child, nobody is liable.

Before 1986, pharmaceutical companies were being sued for billions of dollars in judgments. Who believes they would behave differently having received blanket immunity after 1986? But nowadays, nobody is allowed to look into their affairs.

Even more disturbing is that Congress has allowed vaccines to be fast tracked, so it's very easy to bring them to market. There are no more burdens or impediments on testing, and no more double-blind tests with placebo that a normal drug has to go through. Some vaccines are even brought to market with no testing whatsoever.

As I already pointed out, the 1986 Act launched a gold rush in the vaccine business. Today they have a product that's liability free, and the government is mandating purchase or your kids can't go to school. There's no advertising cost, no marketing cost, no consequences to injuring or hurting anybody. It's an extraordinary product.

Finally, the industry captured the ACIP members with incentives, and that's why there was a rush to add new vaccines to the schedule. And within a few years all the new vaccines appeared on the schedule.

## Tracing the Autism Source

Unfortunately, by using thimerosal as a preservative to maintain long shelf life, that dramatically increased the mercury exposure.

Mercury exposure for a typical American child before age 2 was originally 70 mcg, then it rose to 237 mcg in 1989. Ironically, 1989 was the year the epidemic of neurological disorders began. All the disorders that were rare when I was growing up became ubiquitous; ADD, ADHD, SPEECH DELAY, TICS, ASD, autism, narcolepsy, seizure disorder, antiphylaxis, food allergies, and even asthma.

EPA scientists have identified 1989 as the gateway year that all these unknown diseases suddenly launched. Autism rates that were usually 1 in 2,500 escalated to become 1 in 68 as the vaccination schedule expanded.

The scientific literature clearly associates autism with mercury exposure in fish, in amalgams, in emissions from coal burning power plants, and in vaccines. There are many studies showing that the closer you live to a mercury emitting plant, the higher your chance of having autism. So science knows that mercury is involved in causing autism.

## What's in Those Vaccines?

Everybody knows that mercury in fish is not good to eat. We have advisories for pregnant women to limit their intake of certain fish that contain mercury, which is the cause of various neurological disorders in newborns.

How can we tell mothers not to eat fish because of mercury and yet we inject them, and their babies, with mercury via vaccines? The shot actually has higher mercury content than is found in fish, plus it's directly injected into the blood stream.

The CDC likes to tell this story: ethyl mercury is not as toxic as methyl mercury, because it doesn't have the residency time in the body. In other words, it's eliminated from the body faster, so it doesn't have time to do much damage. But ask to see the scientific studies which validate that, and they never show you anything.

Finally, in 2004, a CDC scientist did a study which supports the argument that ethyl mercury is excreted quickly. It showed ethyl mercury from vaccines disappeared from the blood in 1 week, whereas methyl mercury from fish remained in the blood for 54 days. It was just as the CDC said.

However, that study came under attack by scientists because there was no explanation of how that mercury was excreted. Was it in the feces, sweat, fingernails, hair, or the urine of the vaccinated children? In other words, if it's being excreted from the body we should know where it's going.

About two years later, another scientist was doing studies on macaque monkeys. He fed them methyl mercury and then injected them with the ethyl mercury common in vaccines. He also found that the ethyl mercury did disappear from the moneys very fast.

However, in the autopsies they discovered that it wasn't leaving the body. Rather, it was leaving the blood stream to easily cross the blood/brain barrier and was going directly to the brain. The mercury remained lodged in the brain and that's why it was undetected in the blood.

So, this second study did not validate that ethyl mercury was safe. It revealed an extraordinary danger because it was leaving children's blood stream and going into their brain. The study showed that it metabolized into organic mercury, which is even more toxic causing terrible inflammation and neurological damage.

A few years later, an Italian scientist found that when you compared methyl vs. ethyl mercury, the ethyl was 50 times as toxic as methyl. His study concluded that ethyl mercury in vaccines was twice as persistent and 50 times as toxic as methyl mercury in fish.

As a result of the mercury uproar, the CDC stated that they had taken the thimerosal out and it's no longer present in vaccines. What does that mean? It means that it was injected into children for decades prior to taking it out when later studies found it to be toxic. So,

## What's in Those Vaccines?

vaccines with thimerosal classify as experimental medicine that failed.

Despite the promise that thimerosal was no longer used, trace amounts of it are still found in vaccines. In other words, a trace amount means it doesn't have to be listed as an ingredient.

Many good scientific studies prove that exposing a person to mercury causes mitochondrial disorders and that can trigger autism when some other environmental toxins present. So, mercury is still a primary offender.

Pro-vaxxers say it may be something else, not mercury. Still, we know there must be an environmental toxin to cause an epidemic. Yes, genes can create the vulnerability but they do not cause epidemics. For epidemics there must be an environmental toxin.

We ought to be looking for an environmental toxin from around 1989 with a dramatic exposure across every demographic: urban, rural, whites, blacks, from Cuban Americans in Florida to Inuit in Alaska and everybody in between. The epidemic did not touch the unvaccinated like the Amish and religious exempt groups.

We also have to identify a toxin that affects boys on a 4 to 1 ratio to girls. Some people may say it's glyphosate from Roundup, or another pesticide. They're definitely not good to ingest, but pesticides have been around long before 1989. Other people point to the MMR vaccine we've been giving since the mid '70s. Yes, it may trigger autism but something else is involved which creates a precondition allows other environmental toxins to trigger it.

So the CDC, which is charged to protect public health, is aware of the dangers but tries to convince you it's safe. It's very difficult to convince a person of a fact if the admittance of that fact will diminish one's salary. A lot of our beliefs are colored by self-interest.

**Betraying the Public Trust**

Robert F. Kennedy, Jr. explains that there was a secret meeting in 2002, off campus from the CDC in the remote area of Simpsonwood, Georgia. It was chosen because participants thought it would be restricted from a Freedom of Information Law request. However, they were wrong about that.

There were 75 vaccine producers, key officials from federal agencies: the FDA, CDC, NIH, WHO, and others, present at that meeting to discuss how to handle the mercury information. In the transcript from the Simpsonwood secret meeting, the CDC members realized that mercury was causing the autism epidemic.

The transcript reveals their shock at the mercury discoveries. People were saying things like: *how could this have happened? We were asleep at the wheel. It's childhood math. Why didn't we look at these mercury*

## What's in Those Vaccines?

*loads? Why didn't we do a mass analysis on mercury exposure when we ordered all the new vaccines that were going to be for kids?* And much more. There were a lot of *mea culpas* [my fault].

At that time, it was easy to follow the email trail. Some people wanted to come clean: *we gotta do the right thing, gotta tell the American people, we have to rebuild the credibility of our vaccination program, express our regret,* etc. This is all in the recorded transcript.

On the second day of the meeting, other voices began to insert themselves: *if we admit, the lawyers will come out of the woodwork, we'll be sued,* and so on.

Then, however, they begin to band together. They were telling each other about the dangers of thimerosal in vaccines: *we've gotta hide this, keep it quiet, it's not ambiguous it's real, but we have to conceal it.* It's clear that they knew all along about mercury's toxic effect.

By the end of the second day, however, these public servants came to the conclusion that it's best to hide it from the American people. And that's what they've been doing ever since that day.

The email trail over the next year from IOM, and CDC, was a written record saying how they decided to: *come up with new studies to justify our point of view that will show there's* [sic] *no problems, and no connection to autism.* The transcript shows how people's worst instincts, survival instincts, took over. This is all documented. It's not hearsay.

The CDC had a giant repository of children's health information called the Vaccine Safety Data Base. They spend $20 million every year to maintain this data base. Its goal was precisely for doing epidemiological studies to identify if toxins in vaccines were causing problems.

They had their in-house epidemiologist, Thomas Verstratton. He began looking at the data. His initial runs showed clearly that thimerosal was causing the autism epidemic.

His study looked at the kids who received less than 25 mcg and those who received more than 25 mcg of thimerosal. He found a relative risk (RR) of 760. That equals a 760 percent greater chance for the higher exposed group to get an autism diagnosis.

In one of the runs he even found an RR of 1100. This was greater than the association between smoking a pack of cigarettes every day and cancer. So the CDC staff knew that the mercury in thimerosal was causing the autism epidemic.

### Fudging the Figures

They also found similar associations for ADD, ADHD, TICS, speech delay, and several other neurodevelopmental disorders. Verstratton came under a lot of pressure to change those results. In the email records, he talks about how he's massaging the data but the autism signal continues to persist and "it just won't go away."

After the Simpsonwood meetings there are many emails saying "let's go to other countries with lower exposures of thimerosal and do epidemiological studies." All of these messages from the recorded transcript are FOIA documents, (Freedom of Information Act) as researched by Robert F. Kennedy, Jr.

The IOM had stated that the link between autism and thimerosal in vaccines was "biologically plausible," so they instructed CDC to do a range of toxicological and clinical studies, even animals studies. However, at the time of writing this chapter, the CDC has still not done those studies.

Instead, they did a series of epidemiological studies in countries where the exposure to thimerosal was much less. They took advantage of changing reporting requirements in those countries. For example, thimerosal was banned in Scandinavia in 1993, yet autism levels actually climbed after the ban, so the CDC jumped on this.

Later, it was discovered that the reason the levels climbed was due to an artifact of changing the reporting requirements, not because the incidence of autism was climbing.

Prior to 1993, Denmark had only required in-patient cases (persons permanently hospitalized) of autism to be reported to its national disease registry. Every developed nation has a registry of contagious diseases but autism isn't contagious, so it wasn't reported. But in 1993, it became mandatory to report, which was the same year Denmark banned thimerosal because autism was exploding. That's the reason it looked like the number of cases had increased after thimerosal was banned.

The CDC took advantage of that reporting circumstance. They sent a data manager, named Poul Thorson, to Denmark with a million dollars to do a thimerosal study. Regrettably, that huge sum of money swayed Thorson to abscond with the money and he never did the study.

The FBI and the Justice Department issued a 22-count indictment for fraud and wire theft against him. He's still on the run from Interpol in Europe. Despite all this intrigue, the CDC continues to tout the Denmark case as proof that thimerosal doesn't cause autism. It's like Ripley's, Believe it or Not!

Attorney Robert F. Kennedy, Jr. was involved in investigating the case, so he immediately filed a suit against the CDC to allow him to depose their senior vaccine safety scientist, Dr. William Thompson.

Fortunately, after years of felling guilty, Thompson had a change of heart. He came forth to admit on tape that the CDC had been manipulating and even destroying data in its vaccine studies. In this manner, they were deceiving and defrauding the general public, as well as the public health community, about the safety of thimerosal.

Of course, the CDC is not allowing Dr. Thompson to speak publicly before a grand jury to this day. It's tragically ironic that the CDC slogan is: saving lives and protecting people. But in reality, their practical *modus operandi* is: saving programs and protecting profits.

### Independent Investigations

Brian S. Hooker, PhD, PE, was also involved in the CDC exposé. Hooker is a Bioengineer as well as a Research Scientist. His son became autistic due to an adverse vaccine reaction, so he was trying to get the CDC autism data in their files to analyze it independently.

Dr. William Thompson was one of the CDC research scientists involved in the MMR/autism study relationship, and he knew there was something wrong with the way CDC was analyzing the data. He also knew that Hooker was trying to get that data to independently analyze it. But Thompson was aware that Hooker was going about it the wrong way. So, surreptitiously, he decided to give some guidance to Hooker.

Dr. Hooker explained what happened. "He showed me how to submit a release for a public data set. By law, the CDC when they use federal funds to do a vaccine study they have to come up with a public data set that the general public, and primarily scientists on the outside, can have access to. Through his guidance, by Jan 2014, I was swimming in data that I never knew existed."

From Thompson's guidance on how to use the Freedom of Information Act to get data, Hooker was able to get everything he needed for independent analysis.

In a public interview Hooker explained what motivated Thompson to help him. "He knew the CDC was doing bad statistics and actually lying about the relationship between vaccines and autism." Essentially, Thompson revealed that the CDC was knowingly lying about data relating to vaccines and autism, and his conscience finally got to him.

"He began talking about the flaws in the methodology the CDC was using and then the conversation turned to fraud. I think this had been brewing in his conscience since 2004 when he saw blatant fraud by his superiors at the CDC. And this is what he was reporting, that he wanted to make sure that somebody on the outside knew that this fraud had taken place."

Dr. Thompson's tactic was to allow Hooker to get the data and have Dr. Hooker publish the results in peer reviewed scientific literature that showed there was a relationship between autism and vaccines.

"We started with a study of MMR vaccine that was fraudulent and flawed that he had done in 2004, and he wanted me to re-analyze that data set."

Clearly, Thompson wanted to rectify his previous transgressions. So as the original scientist who was on the research project, he contacted Dr. Hooker and requested him to re-analyze the data and publish it.

"He [Dr. Thompson] was the lead statistician on the study. The first author of the study was Frank deStafano who was, and is, the head of the Immunization Safety Office at the CDC. Coleen Boyle was another author of that study and she's second in command at the CDC, and head of one of the major national centers for birth defects and developmental disabilities.

"They, and two others, colluded to cover up several different alarming results that showed the MMR was more susceptible and more likely to give an autism diagnosis than when you delay it until after 3 years of age."

A question arises at this point. *Why does the CDC recommend giving the MMR so early as part of the Combo 10 before 2 years of age, if they know it has a far less harmful effect if delayed*? This is very suspicious and I hope somebody gets to the bottom of this as soon as possible. Apparently, Dr. Thompson talked about the collusion among CDC scientists to eliminate data from the study to make it appear a certain way.

Dr. Hooker continues his explanation. "He did use the word collude and used strong language to say that the published data was fraudulent. He presented how the study was to be done in the first place, and the steps how they deviated from that plan because they saw relationships between MMR and autism, which they did not want to publish. These conversations were recorded so they are documented and validated as real."

Another question comes to mind at this point. *How many families now have autistic children because the true relationship between autism and the MMR vaccine was kept hidden?* These revelations are exposing a criminal mentality to defraud and harm the public. All because of money? Or is there a hidden agenda that has not been released yet?

"The CDC knew about the MMR/autism relationship as early as Nov 7, 2001, because I have a memo dated Nov 7, 2001 and it delineates these relationships and shows a strong positive relationship with MMR/autism among African Americans, and showed isolated autism."

Isolated autism refers to children that became autistic but had no other kinds of morbidities, like cerebral palsy or mental retardation. In other words, just a basic regression into autism.

"CDC knew about it since Nov/2001, and look at how many kids have been born since then and been damaged by the MMR, and how many shattered families could have been saved from this tragedy.

"Yet if they had delayed giving MMR for some time the risk of autism went down precipitously. They could have said, *we have new data so let's delay the shot*, but it would have meant that the kids that got the earlier shots based on their recommendation now have autism. So, they could not go on record and admit it, so they chose to cover it up.

"They sat on that information for a year and a half while they met weekly to have Thompson manipulate the data, but he could not make the effect go away. So, they decided, for African American families, that they would only rely on race data for those individuals that have a valid state of Georgia birth certificate. In other words, they reduced the population by almost 50%, so with the smaller sample size you lose statistical power, which means you lose the relationship.

"So, Thompson's superiors said, *run it this way and see what happens*. And when they eliminated those kids without a Georgia birth certificate the relationship went away. As if the birth certificate changes the genetics of a child. Why should that matter to the study?"

Clearly, there is no scientific reason that could validate the actions of the CDC scientists. Obviously, scientists are humans that are not free from corruption and fraud. Simply to save face, they reduced the statistical power of the study to make the relationship go away. ==It was a violation of the Federal Records Act of 1950, which is meant to archive federal records, but they destroyed that data.==

"Dr. Thompson knew that he would be legally liable for destroying that information so he retained his own hard copy and the electronic copies on his hard drive, which is what he shared with me. Congressman Posey now has copies of this information, and he wants to call Thompson as a whistleblower to appear in front of Congress and talk about this fraud."

Dr. Thompson is eager to testify before Congress. He hired a whistleblower attorney, and has declared federal whistleblower status, which gives him the protection afforded by that status. He has also contacted Congressman Bill Posey who is sympathetic to the autism/vaccine issue.

Thompson gave Posey mountains of information, thousands of pages of documents, and shared all the records that showed the CDC fraud. Instead of taking the side of changing the vaccine schedule for increased safety, CDC chose to change the vaccine schedule on the side of increased profits for the pharmaceutical industry, and themselves because they also act as a vaccine company.

Dr. Hooker admitted that he didn't let Thompson know that their conversations were being recorded. He justified the surreptitious recording because he wanted proof that confirmed his discussions with a government scientist at the center of the study confessing how senior CDC officials colluded to commit fraud.

Thompson's belief is that vaccine safety doesn't belong with the CDC or the HHS unless they're reformed and become independent from Big Pharma money. It's clear that some people cannot continue cheating beyond a certain point when they have to opt out and say "enough."

Hooker explained that he needed the evidence with a time-stamp that would stand up in a court of law. That's why he retained two attorneys who worked with him to ensure he was not doing anything illegal.

Dr. Hooker questions how many more families need to suffer the heavy risk of complying with a vaccination experiment that has never been properly researched. Moreover, the research that has been done indicates serious danger for families who innocently follow the CDC vaccine schedule.

Nowadays, people assert that the vaccine/autism link has been refuted and scientifically disproven. They are still unaware that the true facts were falsified. Thus, many people bring in their children to comply with the CDC schedule although they have been defrauded.

If families knew that simply by delaying the MMR vaccine until their children were a little older, they could reduce the risk by a large factor. But the CDC didn't even consider that. They chose to dispose of the data in the original study that proved the autism link.

When we consider the lives that could have been saved if the MMR/autism link was made public, it's imperative we clean the CDC house. We need to bring the corrupt scientists to justice. Only complete reform will give some vindication to families that have suffered for decades.

## The Facts Remain Hidden

Thompson's account has now gone through peer review, and nobody has objected to his statistical analysis. Even so, the media won't cover the story. They use the excuse that it will have a negative effect on public health and that shouldn't happen. They say that the truth will have a negative effect on public health so better not tell the truth? That's how advertising revenue can spoil integrity.

Due to the malfeasance at the CDC, the American people have no knowledge about the dangers of vaccination. The first reaction of most people is always, *this couldn't be true.* Or, *why would the CDC lie about vaccine safety*?

I admit it *is* beyond belief, until you read the entire Simpsonwood transcript to understand what actually happened at the CDC. Then it becomes clear why senior public servants chose to protect themselves, and the institution, instead of protecting the millions of children who would be vaccinated year after year.

Of course, this is not unprecedented. One simply has to look at the pedophile scandal in the Catholic Church where some priests were actually raping young boys. People view priests as representing God, and spoiling that trust was not an option. Thus, bishops protected perpetrators believing that protecting the church was more important than protecting children. *To protect the church, we'll deny wrongdoing; we will even deny the truth.*

We see the same scenario with the vaccine program. The CDC got involved with a perverse dynamic similar to that of the Catholic church. Families view doctors as saving lives, so admitting that doctors are giving vaccines that can damage children is an unacceptable conclusion. When health officials make these decisions, they appear to be rational and necessary choices. They don't see themselves as selfish or evil because they are protecting public health. However, when we see it objectively from the outside, it looks horrific.

That's how it became more important to protect a corrupt CDC than to protect innocent children. And this was all justified because the children were seen as sacrificial lambs for the greater public good.

These vaccine revelations capture the social dynamic and the psycho-dynamic showing how people can collectively come to the same line of thinking what's right, and thus trick themselves into believing they are doing something good. Sir Walter Scott said it best: "Oh what a tangled web we weave, when first we practice to deceive."

We've see this rationale throughout history where idealistic people who want to do public service somehow get sucked into a vortex where they justify conduct and behavior to themselves, but which is ultimately socially malevolent.

# ~ 15 ~
# The Future of Vaccines

> No force on Earth can stop an idea whose time has come
>
> - Victor Hugo

The most important outcome to settle the vaccine issue is to arrange a public debate about the issue. The CDC will not be able to withstand a public discussion.

Robert F. Kennedy, Jr. articulates his experience, understanding and vision to bring the vaccine issue out of the darkness of corruption and into the light of open discussion.

"All the things that I do are bent on forcing this debate out into the open. Because once the science is in the open, the CDC's position is so fragile. It's an edifice of fraud stacked upon fraud so high, and so wobbly, that even a slight breeze of public scrutiny will topple it.

"But the genius of what they've been able to do is to stop all that public scrutiny. It's not only Congress that won't investigate them; the regulatory agencies have been captured. The courts and the lawyers that would normally apply that scrutiny have been removed by the Vaccine Act [1986].

"And the press has been compromised. And it's not just the mainstream, corporate media, but also the so-called alternate media like HuffPost and Slade, and Daily Beast [Salon], even Mother Jones, for whom this is a taboo topic. They simply will not cover it. They will not allow editorial, they won't allow letters, they won't allow any discussion. That is really like a Kafkaesque cocoon.

"An article in the *Columbian Journalism Review* stated that, for a journalist this is radioactive, this is a career ending controversy. So, reporters won't touch it. Everybody is scared of it. Doctors can lose their license if they talk about this. The scientific journals won't publish on it because they get directly punished as their revenues are coming largely from pharmaceutical companies.

"So they've effectively been able to shut off any kind of controversy. Mushrooms need darkness in order to flourish and that's what's happened. What we need is sunlight. If you put a little sunlight on this controversy the whole thing is gonna fall apart.

"All of my strategies, the lawsuits, the articles, public statements, demonstrations, everything is about trying to have a debate in our democracy. I've never seen anything like this in my life where you're simply not allowed to talk about it. The only place where talk is going on is on social media, and internet documentaries that will never air on mainstream TV.

"So our only resource left is to get the social media active before they also try to shut that down. But we will win this because all it takes is one crack, like one editor to say, *yes, we're gonna do a series on the corruption at the CDC.*

Or, one producer who decides he doesn't want to be censored anymore and wants to document the story because his family had a bad vaccine experience. Or it could be a judge who looks at the facts and the science and says, *I'm going to allow Dr. William Thompson to be deposed publicly.*

"It could be a congressman who subpoenas Thompson before a committee and exposes the whole thing and forces a debate. As soon as that debate happens the opposition will shrivel. That's what's needed – sunlight. We live in a democracy and it's absolutely insane that we're not allowed to talk about this.

"This phenomenon is not about science. Everything is taken on faith and nobody is allowed to challenge it, debate it. You have to accept the received knowledge of the higher powers, CDC scientists, who already have the proven studies. It's just like any other dogma.

"Where else does the press allow a government agency to tell it what the science says? Why don't reporters actually do the research and read the science to discover the facts for themselves? Because anybody who doesn't accept the dogma will be marginalized, vilified, ridiculed, dismissed, and have their credentials revoked.

"The level of viciousness towards the mothers of vaccine-injured children, or vaccine-hesitant parents, is unprecedented. These parents are not psychopaths or crackpots as they are being labeled. It's a very misogynistic impulse against women who are making complaints, and these women know what happened to their child!

"They bring a healthy child to their pediatrician; get a battery of shots, and that night the baby has a fever, maybe a seizure, and over the next few weeks regresses into autistic behavior. This has never happened in history before. There's no record of such events prior to the 20th century where normal children suddenly regressed into intellectual disability.

"Mothers who understood what happened are being dismissed as hysterical crackpots. Thousands of mothers are being dismissed and pejorative language is used against them. Nobody is listening to their stories and discovering how to solve the problem.

"This is the response of modern doctors to intelligent women who are well-informed and know the science, because they've read the government documents, the Simpsonwood transcripts, and attended many meetings. They weren't anti-vaccine because they vaccinated their kid and saw what happened. That's what goes on with dogma, not with science. Every dogma is ultimately cruel and even ruthless because they never consider another viewpoint, and never allow any questioning.

"When doctors just do what they're told to do that's not Science because science is not dogma. You have to allow the questions, and you can't just believe in it no matter what. There's 100 million kids a year being poisoned and exposed to this harm through thimerosal in vaccines.

"The depth of what has happened to kids really shakes me to the core and what will happen to future generations? What do we need to do to turn the tide? Write letters to your member of congress, to your newspaper, even to President Trump because he is interested in solving this scandal.

"We need the media to start covering this issue honestly because the process behind the entire vaccine fiasco is how we can make money from vaccinations. It's definitely not about health. And it's not only about the children but also about our military where we vaccinate all our troops. It's about the fraud, the corruption, and the greed.

"It's all down to saving money rather than saving lives. It's the manufacturers that have caused this tragedy by cutting corners and losing public trust. If they hadn't been so greedy, we could have had safe vaccines. They have dug this pit with their own dishonesty.

"When are those responsible going to be called to account for their ignorance, criminal complicity, conflict of interests, and grievous bodily harm?

## Autism

"When you have a protocol and you get data, and then you don't like the data you got so then you go back and change the rules, that's fraud in anybody's book."

Today the CDC functions as a profit-making company instead of a health-protecting agency. They take taxpayer dollars to buy vaccines from the drug companies. By distributing those vaccines through state public health departments, they profit from that distribution. In other words, if vaccine sales decline the CDC will lose money. Thus, there is a conflict of interest to ensure that vaccine sales increase rather than ensure that vaccines become safer and more effective.

The CDC slogan, "saving lives and protecting people" has regressed into, "saving programs and protecting profits."

Dr. Larry Palevsky explains that he started medical school 1983, but it wasn't until 1998 that a mother came to him and asked, "Dr. Larry, did you know that there's mercury in vaccines?"

Many doctors push such questions aside with the common retort, *it's such a small amount, it doesn't matter.* He admitted that that he didn't know, but that motivated him to begin research to see what else was in vaccines. "I realized," he explained, "that there's a great amount of material in vaccines that impairs many cell structures and cell functions."

Dr. Humphries concurs that most doctors are uninformed, and therefore they cannot give informed counsel. In her research she found that vaccines "can have tumorigenic kidney cells of a cocker spaniel in it. It can have human fetal cells with retroviruses."

And most vaccines also have aluminum, which she claims, "is one of the most horrible things to inject into any sort of life form, especially into a muscle."

She candidly admits that, "Parents really need to know that their doctors are not informed, therefore they cannot give informed consent." This is a major reason why parents "really need to think about it because you cannot un-vaccinate."

It's appalling that doctors don't know what's in the vaccines they dispense. When you show them the printed ingredient insert and ask what each one does, they have no idea.

Documentary and Television producer, Del Bigtree explains that his mechanic can tell him about all the different fluids in his car, the viscosity of motor oil and transmission fluid, why they are different, and what they do to benefit the drive train of a car.

A baker can tell you every ingredient he used for the cake, which ones were stirred, mixed, or folded, the optimum temperature of the oven to bake a cake, an apple pie, or a pizza, and how many minutes you bake for each to be ready. Every person you speak to knows everything about their business, except doctors injecting vaccines!

If that's not bad enough, statistics show that the third leading cause of death in America is hospitals themselves. Between 250,000 and 400,000 people die in hospitals every year in the U.S. They're not dying from the illness they went to the hospital for treatment. Rather, they are killed by medical mistakes, bacterial infections that can't be stopped, and other medical malpractice concerns.

Compare these yearly figures with the 65,000 soldiers who died fighting in the Vietnam war, which caused demonstrations and marches in the streets when the '60s erupted against America's involvement in Vietnam. Yet today, 250,000 - 400,000 people die in hospitals from some form of medical malpractice every year and nobody does anything about it.

## Empowerment Through Education

Historical evidence shows that vaccines are not the answer to disease. There is always the fear that your child may get a disease, so the history is really important because we should know under what conditions a child becomes susceptible. Although measles does spread rapidly through a population, it actually benefits the body with lifelong immunity, and that knowledge is more important than transmission.

Dr. Suzanne Humphries notes that the human body is designed in such a perfect way that there's a system in place to handle just about anything that comes along. Of course, as long as we provide the body with proper nutrition, exercise and rest.

"Babies who come into this world in a normal and natural way, who are breastfed for an appropriate amount of time, that's the best protection you could ever give to your baby's immune system or brain. Consider that, when fear starts to creep in. If you breastfeed your baby, you're already giving the most powerful thing on the planet that can be given to that baby," she asserts.

Dr. Joseph Mercola corroborates this understanding.

"There's just no question that improving your innate immune system – through reducing sugar and processed foods in your diet, improving your gut flora, leading a healthy lifestyle, and having adequate vitamin D levels, ideally through sensible sun exposure – will provide a far more effective immune response, and virtually eliminate any risk of developing a life-threatening infection. The key is to have the courage to trust in this truth, that your body is designed to maintain health."

Dr. Humphries adds to Dr. Mercola's assessment with a blatant truth.

"We have a highly profitable, lucrative religion that involves the government, industry, and academia. That religion is vaccination. People believe in vaccines. They'll tell you, they believe in vaccines. But you ask them what they know about vaccines and it will be almost nothing.

"Medical schools are bereft of information on the history of vaccination, on the contents of them, and the potential problems.

"Doctors are really being systematically brainwashed. Not only that, but if doctors do start to see problems... wake up to it; do their own research, and buck the system, they risk being treated the way I was. I was well respected through the entire state of Maine. People were referring their patients to me. My colleagues would come to me with their medical problems... But once I started to argue against the practice of vaccination, I was automatically tossed into the category of a quack..."

For a highly informative read, Dr. Humphries's book *Dissolving Illusions: Disease, Vaccines, and the*

# The Future of Vaccines

*Forgotten History* is available on Amazon. Or you can visit her website, dissolvingillusions.com, for more information on vaccination.

Science Researcher Mike Adams is confident about the future of medicine. He says it "will not involve injecting children with toxic chemicals and calling it immunization. There is a much better way to protect the lives of children and I want to help that future arrive more quickly. I want to advance medicine. I want to see medicine progress past the dark ages under which it operates today."

Again, natural immunity is lifelong and acquired immunity is temporary, because vaccination requires booster shots at regular intervals as the immunity continually decreases.

We live in a time when ethical scientists have to become whistleblowers, and are even threatened with violence by vaccine industry operators and biotech industry insiders. We live in dangerous times but intimidation will not force us into silence.

Big Pharma has tried many strategies to stop the movement against mandatory vaccination. They will never be successful because mothers are driven by a divine mission to protect their children. Their spirit is bulletproof, as it should be.

Nobody can kill an idea whose time has come by utilizing intimidation or violence. No one can kill the truth with threats. Every revealed truth will continue to live into the future. Our fight for truth lives on after we are gone.

So, the future is bright because families will win and Big Pharma will lose just like Big Tobacco lost. It's only a matter of time before the light of truth illuminates and exposes the corruption.

# Another book by this author

## Cosmology on Trial: Cracking the Cosmic Code

Amazon Bestselling author, Pierre St. Clair, examines present models of the universe like an attorney in a court of law, without complex jargon.

The author's manner is, "Just the facts please. Show me the evidence."

**Cosmology on Trial** presents the remarkable findings of his study and introduces readers to unexplained and unsolved mysteries of the universe.

Please copy this link: http://amzn.to/1UBj5ni into your browser to see the book on Amazon.com.

Thank you,

Open Mind Publishers

# ~ 16 ~
# Appendix

> I've heard of many tragic cases of walking, talking normal children who wound up with profound mental disorders after vaccines.
>
> - Rand Paul, M.D.

The Nuremburg Code of August 1947

1. The voluntary consent of the human subject is absolutely essential. This means that the person involved should have legal capacity to give consent; should be so situated as to be able to exercise free power of choice, without the intervention of any element of force, fraud, deceit, duress, over-reaching, or other ulterior form of constraint or coercion; and

should have sufficient knowledge and comprehension of the elements of the subject matter involved, as to enable him to make an understanding and enlightened decision.

This latter element requires that, before the acceptance of an affirmative decision by the experimental subject, there should be made known to him the nature, duration, and purpose of the experiment; the method and means by which it is to be conducted; all inconveniences and hazards reasonably to be expected; and the effects upon his health or person, which may possibly come from his participation in the experiment.

The duty and responsibility for ascertaining the quality of the consent rests upon each individual who initiates, directs or engages in the experiment. It is a personal duty and responsibility which may not be delegated to another with impunity.

2. The experiment should be such as to yield fruitful results for the good of society, unprocurable by other methods or means of study, and not random and unnecessary in nature.

3. The experiment should be so designed and based on the results of animal experimentation and a knowledge of the natural history of the disease or other problem under study, that the anticipated results will justify the performance of the experiment.

4. The experiment should be so conducted as to avoid all unnecessary physical and mental suffering and injury.

5. No experiment should be conducted, where there is an a priori reason to believe that death or disabling

injury will occur; except, perhaps, in those experiments where the experimental physicians also serve as subjects.

6. The degree of risk to be taken should never exceed that determined by the humanitarian importance of the problem to be solved by the experiment.

7. Proper preparations should be made and adequate facilities provided to protect the experimental subject against even remote possibilities of injury, disability, or death.

8. The experiment should be conducted only by scientifically qualified persons. The highest degree of skill and care should be required through all stages of the experiment of those who conduct or engage in the experiment.

9. During the course of the experiment, the human subject should be at liberty to bring the experiment to an end, if he has reached the physical or mental state, where continuation of the experiment seemed to him to be impossible.

10. During the course of the experiment, the scientist in charge must be prepared to terminate the experiment at any stage, if he has probable cause to believe, in the exercise of the good faith, superior skill and careful judgement required of him, that a continuation of the experiment is likely to result in injury, disability, or death to the experimental subject.

["Trials of War Criminals before the Nuremberg Military Tribunals under Control Council Law No. 10", Vol. 2, pp. 181-182. Washington, D.C.: U.S. Government Printing Office, 1949.]

Dr. Tetyana's letter sent to California legislators prior to their vote on SB 277

An Open Letter to Legislators Currently Considering Vaccine Legislation from Tetyana Obukhanych, PhD in Immunology

Re: VACCINE LEGISLATION

Dear Legislator:

My name is Tetyana Obukhanych. I hold a PhD in Immunology. I am writing this letter in the hope that it will correct several common misperceptions about vaccines in order to help you formulate a fair and balanced understanding that is supported by accepted vaccine theory and new scientific findings.

Do unvaccinated children pose a higher threat to the public than the vaccinated?

It is often stated that those who choose not to vaccinate their children for reasons of conscience endanger the rest of the public, and this is the rationale behind most of the legislation to end vaccine

# Appendix

exemptions currently being considered by federal and state legislators country-wide.

You should be aware that the nature of protection afforded by many modern vaccines – and that includes most of the vaccines recommended by the CDC for children – is not consistent with such a statement. I have outlined below the recommended vaccines that cannot prevent transmission of disease either because they are not *designed* to prevent the transmission of infection (rather, they are intended to prevent disease symptoms), or because they are for non-communicable diseases.

People who have not received the vaccines mentioned below pose no higher threat to the general public than those who have, implying that discrimination against non-immunized children in a public-school setting may not be warranted.

1. **IPV (inactivated poliovirus vaccine) cannot prevent transmission of poliovirus** (see appendix for the scientific study, Item #1). Wild poliovirus has been non-existent in the USA for at least two decades. Even if wild poliovirus were to be re-imported by travel, vaccinating for polio with IPV cannot affect the safety of public spaces. Please note that wild poliovirus eradication is attributed to the use of a different vaccine, OPV or oral poliovirus vaccine. Despite being capable of preventing wild poliovirus transmission, use of OPV was phased out long

ago in the USA and replaced with IPV due to safety concerns.
2. **Tetanus is not a contagious disease**, but rather acquired from deep-puncture wounds contaminated with *C. tetani* spores. Vaccinating for tetanus (via the DTaP combination vaccine) cannot alter the safety of public spaces; it is intended to render personal protection only.
3. While intended to prevent the disease-causing effects of the diphtheria toxin, **the diphtheria toxoid vaccine** (also contained in the DTaP vaccine) **is not designed to prevent colonization and transmission of *C. diphtheriae*.** Vaccinating for diphtheria cannot alter the safety of public spaces; it is likewise intended for personal protection only.
4. The acellular pertussis (aP) vaccine (the final element of the DTaP combined vaccine), now in use in the USA, replaced the whole cell pertussis vaccine in the late 1990s, which was followed by an unprecedented resurgence of whooping cough. An experiment with deliberate pertussis infection in primates revealed that **the aP vaccine is not capable of preventing colonization and transmission of *B. pertussis*** (see appendix for the scientific study, Item #2). The FDA has issued a warning regarding this crucial finding. [1]
5. Furthermore, the 2013 meeting of the Board of Scientific Counselors at the CDC revealed

additional alarming data that pertussis variants (PRN-negative strains) currently circulating in the USA acquired a selective advantage to infect those who are up-to-date for their DTaP boosters (see appendix for the CDC document, Item #3), meaning that people who are up-to-date are *more* likely to be infected, and thus contagious, than people who are not vaccinated.

6. Among numerous types of *H. influenzae*, the Hib vaccine covers only type b. Despite its sole intention to reduce symptomatic and asymptomatic (disease-less) Hib carriage, **the introduction of the Hib vaccine has inadvertently shifted strain dominance towards other types of *H. influenzae*** (types a through f).

7. These types have been causing invasive disease of high severity and increasing incidence in adults in the era of Hib vaccination of children (see appendix for the scientific study, Item #4). The general population is more vulnerable to the invasive disease now than it was prior to the start of the Hib vaccination campaign. Discriminating against children who are not vaccinated for Hib does not make any scientific sense in the era of non-type b *H. influenzae* disease.

8. **Hepatitis B is a blood-borne virus.** It does not spread in a community setting, especially among children who are unlikely to engage in high-risk behaviors, such as needle sharing or

sex. Vaccinating children for hepatitis B cannot significantly alter the safety of public spaces. Further, school admission is not prohibited for children who are chronic hepatitis B carriers. To prohibit school admission for those who are simply unvaccinated – and do not even carry hepatitis B – would constitute unreasonable and illogical discrimination.

In summary, a person who is not vaccinated with IPV, DTaP, HepB, and Hib vaccines due to reasons of conscience, poses no extra danger to the public than a person who is. No discrimination is warranted.

How often do serious vaccine adverse events happen?

It is often stated that vaccination rarely leads to serious adverse events. Unfortunately, this statement is not supported by science. A recent study done in Ontario, Canada, established that, *vaccination actually leads to an emergency room visit for 1 in 168 children following their 12-month vaccination appointment and for 1 in 730 children following their 18-month vaccination appointment* (see appendix for a scientific study, Item #5).

When the risk of an adverse event requiring an ER visit after well-baby vaccinations is demonstrably so high, vaccination must remain a choice for parents, who may understandably be unwilling to assume this immediate risk in order to protect their children from diseases that are generally considered mild or that their children may never be exposed to.

Can discrimination against families who oppose vaccines for reasons of conscience prevent future disease outbreaks of communicable viral diseases, such as measles?

Measles research scientists have for a long time been aware of the "measles paradox." I quote from the article by Poland & Jacobson (1994) "**Failure to Reach the Goal of Measles Elimination: Apparent Paradox of Measles Infections in Immunized Persons.**" *Arch Intern Med* 154:1815-1820:

"**THE APPARENT PARADOX IS THAT AS MEASLES IMMUNIZATION RATES RISE TO HIGH LEVELS IN A POPULATION, MEASLES BECOMES A DISEASE OF IMMUNIZED PERSONS.**" [2]

Further research determined that behind the "measles paradox" is a fraction of the population called LOW VACCINE RESPONDERS. Low-responders are those who respond poorly to the first dose of the measles vaccine. These individuals then mount a weak immune response to subsequent RE-vaccination and quickly return to the pool of "susceptibles" within 2-5 years, despite being fully vaccinated. [3]

Re-vaccination cannot correct low-responsiveness: it appears to be an immuno-genetic trait. [4]

The proportion of low-responders among children was estimated to be 4.7% in the USA. [5]

Studies of measles outbreaks in Quebec, Canada, and China attest that *outbreaks of measles still happen, even when vaccination compliance is in the highest bracket* (95-97% or even 99%, see appendix for scientific studies, Items #6&7). This is because even in high vaccine responders, vaccine-induced antibodies wane over time. Vaccine immunity does not equal life-long immunity acquired after natural exposure.

It has been documented that vaccinated persons who develop breakthrough measles are contagious. In fact, two major measles outbreaks in 2011 (in Quebec, Canada, and in New York, NY) were re-imported by previously vaccinated individuals. [6] – [7]

Taken together, these data make it apparent that elimination of vaccine exemptions, currently only utilized by a small percentage of families anyway, will neither solve the problem of disease resurgence nor prevent re-importation and outbreaks of previously eliminated diseases.

Is discrimination against conscientious vaccine objectors the only practical solution?

The majority of measles cases in recent US outbreaks (including the recent Disneyland outbreak) are adults and very young babies, whereas in the pre-vaccination era, measles occurred mainly between the ages 1 and 15. Natural exposure to measles was followed by lifelong immunity from re-infection, whereas vaccine immunity wanes over time, leaving adults unprotected by their childhood shots. Measles is more dangerous for infants and for adults than for school-aged children.

Despite high chances of exposure in the pre-vaccination era, measles practically never happened in babies much younger than one year of age due to the robust maternal immunity transfer mechanism. The vulnerability of very young babies to measles today is the direct outcome of the prolonged mass vaccination campaign of the past, during which their mothers, themselves vaccinated in their childhood, were not able to experience measles naturally at a safe school age and establish the lifelong immunity that would also be transferred to their babies and protect them from measles for the first year of life.

Luckily, a therapeutic backup exists to mimic now-eroded maternal immunity. Infants as well as other vulnerable or immunocompromised individuals, **are eligible to receive immunoglobulin, a potentially life-saving measure that supplies antibodies directed against the virus to prevent or ameliorate disease upon exposure** (appendix, Item #8).

In summary:

1) due to the properties of modern vaccines, non-vaccinated individuals pose no greater risk of transmission of polio, diphtheria, pertussis, and numerous non-type b *H. influenzae* strains than

vaccinated individuals do, non-vaccinated individuals pose virtually no danger of transmission of hepatitis B in a school setting, and tetanus is not transmissible at all;

2) there is a significantly elevated risk of emergency room visits after childhood vaccination appointments attesting that vaccination is not risk-free;

3) outbreaks of measles cannot be entirely prevented even if we had nearly perfect vaccination compliance; and

4) an effective method of preventing measles and other viral diseases in vaccine-ineligible infants and the immunocompromised, immunoglobulin, is available for those who may be exposed to these diseases.

Taken together, these four facts make it clear that discrimination in a public-school setting against children who are not vaccinated for reasons of conscience is completely unwarranted as the vaccine status of conscientious objectors poses no undue public health risk.

Sincerely Yours,

Tetyana Obukhanych, PhD

Appendix

ITEM #1

The Cuba IPV Study collaborative group. (2007) **Randomized controlled trial of inactivated poliovirus vaccine in Cuba**. N Engl J Med 356:1536-44

http://www.ncbi.nlm.nih.gov/pubmed/17429085

The table below from the Cuban IPV study documents that 91% of children receiving no IPV (control group B) were colonized with live attenuated poliovirus upon deliberate experimental inoculation. Children who were vaccinated with IPV (groups A and C) were similarly colonized at the rate of 94-97%. High counts of live virus were recovered from the stool of children in all groups. These results make it clear that IPV cannot be relied upon for the control of polioviruses.

Table 3. Isolation of Poliovirus in Stool Samples 1 Week after Oral Poliovirus Vaccine Challenge According to Study Group and Poliovirus Type.*

| Group† | No. of Infants | Type 1 | | Type 2 | | Type 3 | | Any Type of Poliovirus | | |
|---|---|---|---|---|---|---|---|---|---|---|
| | | No. | % (95% CI) | No. | % (95% CI) | No. | % (95% CI) | No. | % (95% CI) | Mean Log$_{10}$ Titer in Fecal Sample (95% CI)‡ |
| A | 52 | 10 | 19 (10–33) | 45 | 87 (74–94) | 5 | 10 (3–21) | 49 | 94 (84–99) | 3.46 (3.17–3.75) |
| B | 54 | 9 | 17 (8–29) | 48 | 89 (77–96) | 3 | 6 (1–15) | 49 | 91 (80–97) | 3.89 (3.64–4.14) |
| C | 72 | 13 | 18 (10–29) | 67 | 93 (85–98) | 10 | 14 (7–24) | 70 | 97 (90–100) | 3.37 (3.14–3.60) |

* All stool samples taken from study participants just before the challenge dose were negative for poliovirus. Exact confidence intervals (CIs) are based on the binomial distribution.
† Group A received a combination of diphtheria–pertussis–tetanus vaccine, Haemophilus influenzae type b vaccine, and inactivated poliovirus vaccine (DPT-Hib-IPV) at 6, 10, and 14 weeks of age. Group B, the control group, received a combination of DPT vaccine and Hib vaccine at 6, 10, and 14 weeks. Group C received the DPT-Hib-IPV combination at 8 and 16 weeks.
‡ Mean values are given for excretors of poliovirus.

ITEM #2

Warfel et al. (2014) Acellular pertussis vaccines protect against disease but fail to prevent infection and transmission in a nonhuman primate model. *Proc Natl Acad Sci USA* 111:787-92

http://www.ncbi.nlm.nih.gov/pubmed/24277828

"Baboons vaccinated with aP were protected from severe pertussis-associated symptoms but not from colonization, did not clear the infection faster than naïve [unvaccinated] animals, and readily transmitted B. pertussis to unvaccinated contacts. By comparison, previously infected [naturally-immune] animals were not colonized upon secondary infection."

ITEM #3

Meeting of the Board of Scientific Counselors, Office of Infectious Diseases, Centers for Disease Control and Prevention, Tom Harkins Global Communication Center, Atlanta, Georgia, December 11-12, 2013

http://www.cdc.gov/maso/facm/pdfs/BSCOID/2013 121112_BSCOID_Minutes.pdf

Resurgence of Pertussis (p.6)

"Findings indicated that 85% of the isolates [from six Enhanced Pertussis Surveillance Sites and from epidemics in Washington and Vermont in 2012] were PRN-deficient and vaccinated patients had significantly higher odds than unvaccinated patients of being infected with PRN-deficient strains. Moreover, when patients with up-to-date DTaP vaccinations were compared to unvaccinated patients, the odds of being infected with PRN-deficient strains increased, suggesting that PRN-bacteria may have a selective advantage in infecting DTaP-vaccinated persons."

ITEM #4

Rubach *et al.* (2011) Increasing incidence of invasive *Haemophilus influenzae* disease in adults, Utah, USA. *Emerg Infect Dis* 17:1645-50

http://www.ncbi.nlm.nih.gov/pubmed/21888789

The chart below from Rubach *et al.* shows the number of invasive cases of *H. influenzae* (all types) in Utah in the decade of childhood vaccination for Hib.

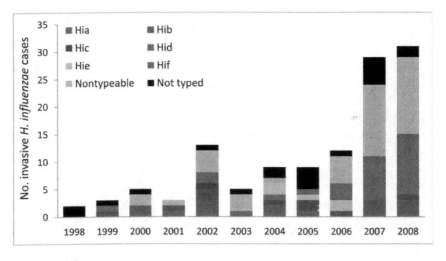

ITEM #5

Wilson *et al.* (2011) Adverse events following 12 and 18-month vaccinations: a population-based, self-controlled case series analysis. *PLoS One* 6:e27897

http://www.ncbi.nlm.nih.gov/pubmed/22174753

"Four to 12 days post 12-month vaccination, children had a 1.33 (1.29-1.38) increased relative incidence of the combined endpoint compared to the control period, or at least one event during the risk interval for every 168 children vaccinated. Ten to 12 days post 18-month vaccination, the relative incidence was 1.25 (95%, 1.17-1.33) which represented at least one excess event for every 730 children vaccinated. The primary reason for increased events was statistically significant elevations in emergency room visits following all vaccinations."

ITEM #6

De Serres *et al.* (2013) Largest measles epidemic in North America in a decade–Quebec, Canada, 2011: contribution of susceptibility, serendipity, and superspreading events. *J Infect Dis* 207:990-98

http://www.ncbi.nlm.nih.gov/pubmed/23264672

"The largest measles epidemic in North America in the last decade occurred in 2011 in Quebec, Canada."

"A super-spreading event triggered by 1 importation resulted in sustained transmission and 678 cases."

"The index case patient was a 30-39-year old adult, after returning to Canada from the Caribbean. The index case patient received measles vaccine in childhood."

"Provincial [Quebec] vaccine coverage surveys conducted in 2006, 2008, and 2010 consistently showed that by 24 months of age, approximately 96% of children had received 1 dose and approximately 85% had received 2 doses of measles vaccine, increasing to 97% and 90%, respectively, by 28 months of age. With additional first and second doses administered between 28 and 59 months of age, population measles vaccine coverage is even higher by school entry."

"Among adolescents, 22% [of measles cases] had received 2 vaccine doses. Outbreak investigation showed this proportion to have been an underestimate; active case finding identified 130% more cases among 2-dose recipients."

ITEM #7

Wang *et al.* (2014) Difficulties in eliminating measles and controlling rubella and mumps: a cross-sectional study of a first measles and rubella vaccination and a second measles, mumps, and rubella vaccination. *PLoS One* 9:e89361

http://www.ncbi.nlm.nih.gov/pubmed/24586717

"The reported coverage of the measles-mumps-rubella (MMR) vaccine is greater than 99.0% in Zhejiang province. However, the incidence of measles, mumps, and rubella remains high."

Item #8. Immunoglobulin Handbook, Health Protection Agency

http://webarchive.nationalarchives.gov.uk/20140714084352/http://www.hpa.org.uk/webc/HPAwebFile/HPAweb_C/1242198450982

HUMAN NORMAL IMMUNOGLOBULIN (HNIG):

Indications

1. To prevent or attenuate an attack in immuno-compromised contacts
2. To prevent or attenuate an attack in pregnant women
3. To prevent or attenuate an attack in infants under the age of 9 months

[1] http://www.fda.gov/NewsEvents/Newsroom/PressAnnouncements/ucm376937.htm

[2] http://archinte.jamanetwork.com/article.aspx?articleid=619215

[3] Poland (1998) *Am J Hum Genet* 62:215-220

http://www.ncbi.nlm.nih.gov/pubmed/9463343

"'poor responders,' who were re-immunized and developed poor or low-level antibody responses only to lose detectable antibody and develop measles on exposure 2–5 years later."

[4] *ibid*

"Our ongoing studies suggest that zero negativity after vaccination [for measles] clusters among related family members, that genetic polymorphisms within the HLA [genes] significantly influence antibody levels."

[5] LeBaron *et al.* (2007) *Arch Pediatr Adolesc Med* 161:294-301

http://www.ncbi.nlm.nih.gov/pubmed/17339511

"Titers fell significantly over time [after second MMR] for the study population overall and, by the final collection, 4.7% of children were potentially susceptible."

[6] De Serres *et al.* (2013) *J Infect Dis* 207:990-998

http://www.ncbi.nlm.nih.gov/pubmed/23264672

"The index case patient received measles vaccine in childhood."

[7] **Rosen *et al.* (2014) *Clin Infect Dis* 58:1205-1210**

http://www.ncbi.nlm.nih.gov/pubmed/24585562

"The index patient had 2 doses of measles-containing vaccine."

Vaccines on Trial

# ~ 17 ~
# CDC Excipient Table

> Immunization is total nonsense. More than that is what's hidden from people about vaccines. They are dangerous. One child out of five has overwhelming disabilities from vaccines - neurological problems, seizures.
>
> - Guylaine Lanctot, M.D.

**Vaccine Excipient & Media Summary**

In addition to weakened or killed disease antigens (viruses or bacteria), vaccines contain very small amounts of other ingredients – excipients or media. Some excipients are added to a vaccine for a specific purpose. These include:

**Preservatives**, to prevent contamination. For example, thimerosal.

**Adjuvants**, to help stimulate a stronger immune response. For example, aluminum salts.

**Stabilizers**, to keep the vaccine potent during transportation and storage. For example, sugars or gelatin.

Others are residual trace amounts of materials that were used during the manufacturing process and removed. These include:

**Cell culture materials**, used to grow the vaccine antigens. For example, egg protein and various culture media.

**Inactivating ingredients**, used to kill viruses or inactivate toxins. For example, formaldehyde.

**Antibiotics**, used to prevent contamination by bacteria. For example, neomycin.

The following table lists all components, other than antigens, shown in the manufacturers' package insert (PI) for each vaccine. Each of these PIs, which can be found on the FDA's website (see below) contains a description of that vaccine's manufacturing process, including the amount and purpose of each substance. In most PIs, this information is found in Section 11: "Description."

All information was extracted from manufacturers' package inserts, current as of January 6, 2017.

If in doubt about whether a PI has been updated since then, check the FDA's website at: http://www.fda.gov/BiologicsBloodVaccines/

## Excipients Included in U.S. Vaccines.

| Vaccine | Contains |
|---|---|
| Adenovirus | human-diploid fibroblast cell cultures (strain WI-38), Dulbecco's Modified Eagle's Medium, fetal bovine serum, sodium bicarbonate, monosodium glutamate, sucrose, D-mannose, D-fructose, dextrose, human serum albumin, potassium phosphate, plasdone C, anhydrous lactose, microcrystalline cellulose, polacrilin potassium, magnesium stearate, microcrystalline cellulose, magnesium stearate, cellulose acetate phthalate, alcohol, acetone, castor oil, FD&C Yellow #6 aluminum lake dye |
| Anthrax (Biothrax) | amino acids, vitamins, inorganic salts, sugars, aluminum hydroxide, sodium chloride, benzethonium chloride, formaldehyde |
| BCG (Tice) | glycerin, asparagine, citric acid, potassium phosphate, magnesium sulfate, iron ammonium citrate, lactose |
| Cholera (Vaxchora) | casamino acids, yeast extract, mineral salts, anti-foaming agent, |

| | |
|---|---|
| | ascorbic acid, hydrolyzed casein, sodium chloride, sucrose, dried lactose, sodium bicarbonate, sodium carbonate |
| DT (Sanofi) | aluminum phosphate, isotonic sodium chloride, formaldehyde, casein, cystine, maltose, uracil, inorganic salts, vitamins, dextrose |
| DTaP (Daptacel) | aluminum phosphate, formaldehyde, glutaraldehyde, 2-phenoxyethanol, Stainer-Scholte medium, casamino acids, dimethyl-beta-cyclodextrin, Mueller's growth medium, ammonium sulfate, modified Mueller-Miller casamino acid medium without beef heart infusion, 2-phenoxyethanol |
| DTaP (Infanrix) | Fenton medium containing a bovine extract, modified Latham medium derived from bovine casein, formaldehyde, modified Stainer-Scholte liquid medium, glutaraldehyde, aluminum hydroxide, sodium chloride, polysorbate 80 (Tween 80) |
| DTaP-IPV (Kinrix) | Fenton medium containing a bovine extract, modified Latham medium derived from bovine |

## CDC Excipient Table

| | |
|---|---|
| | casein, formaldehyde, modified Stainer-Scholte liquid medium, glutaraldehyde, aluminum hydroxide, VERO cells, a continuous line of monkey kidney cells, Calf serum, lactalbumin hydrolysate, sodium chloride, polysorbate 80 (Tween 80), neomycin sulfate, polymyxin B |
| DTaP-IP (Quadracel) | modified Mueller's growth medium, ammonium sulfate, modified Mueller-Miller casamino acid medium without beef heart infusion, formaldehyde, ammonium sulfate aluminum phosphate, Stainer-Scholte medium, casamino acids, dimethyl-beta-cyclodextrin, MRC-5 cells, normal human diploid cells, CMRL 1969 medium supplemented with calf serum, Medium 199 without calf serum, 2-phenoxyethanol, polysorbate 80, glutaraldehyde, neomycin, polymyxin B sulfate |
| DTaP-HepB-IPV (Pediarix) | Fenton medium containing a bovine extract, modified Latham medium derived from bovine casein, |

formaldehyde, modified Stainer-Scholte liquid medium, VERO cells, a continuous line of monkey kidney cells, calf serum and lactalbumin hydrolysate, aluminum hydroxide, aluminum phosphate, aluminum salts, sodium chloride, polysorbate 80 (Tween 80), neomycin sulfate, polymyxin B, yeast protein.

DTaP-IPV/Hib (Pentacel)

aluminum phosphate, polysorbate 80, sucrose, formaldehyde, glutaraldehyde, bovine serum albumin, 2-phenoxyethanol, neomycin, polymyxin B sulfate, modified Mueller's growth medium, ammonium sulfate, modified Mueller-Miller casamino acid medium without beef heart infusion, Stainer-Scholte medium, casamino acids, dimethyl-beta-cyclodextrin, glutaraldehyde,

MRC-5 cells (a line of normal human diploid

## CDC Excipient Table

| | |
|---|---|
| | cells), CMRL 1969 medium supplemented with calf serum, Medium 199 without calf serum, modified Mueller and Miller medium |
| Hib (ActHIB) | sodium chloride, modified Mueller and Miller medium (the culture medium contains milk-derived raw materials [casein derivatives]), formaldehyde, sucrose |
| Hib (Hiberix) | saline, synthetic medium, formaldehyde, sodium chloride, lactose |
| Hib (PedvaxHIB) | complex fermentation media, amorphous aluminum hydroxyphosphate sulfate, sodium chloride |
| Hib/Mening.CY (MenHibrix) | saline, semi-synthetic media, formaldehyde, sucrose, tris (trometamol)-HCl |
| Hep A (Havrix) | MRC-5 human diploid cells, formalin, aluminum hydroxide, amino acid supplement, phosphate-buffered saline solution, |

| | |
|---|---|
| | polysorbate 20, neomycin sulfate, aminoglycoside antibiotic |
| Hep A (Vaqta) | MRC-5 diploid fibroblasts, amorphous aluminum hydroxyl-phosphate sulfate, non-viral protein, DNA, bovine albumin, formaldehyde, neomycin, sodium borate, sodium chloride |
| Hep B (Engerix-B) | aluminum hydroxide, yeast protein, sodium chloride, disodium phosphate dihydrate, sodium dihydrogen phosphate dihydrate |
| Hep B (Recombivax) | soy peptone, dextrose, amino acids, mineral salts, phosphate buffer, formaldehyde, potassium aluminum sulfate, amorphous aluminum hydroxyphosphate sulfate, yeast protein |
| Hep A/Hep B (Twinrix) | MRC-5 human diploid cells, formalin, aluminum phosphate, aluminum hydroxide, amino acids, sodium chloride, phosphate buffer, |

## CDC Excipient Table

| | |
|---|---|
| | polysorbate 20, neomycin sulfate, yeast protein |
| Human Papillomavirus (HPV) (Gardasil) | vitamins, amino acids, mineral salts, carbohydrates, amorphous aluminum hydroxyphosphate sulfate, sodium chloride, L-histidine, polysorbate 80, sodium borate, yeast protein |
| Human Papillomavirus (HPV) (Gardasil 9) | vitamins, amino acids, mineral salts, carbohydrates, amorphous aluminum hydroxyphosphate sulfate, sodium chloride, L-histidine, polysorbate 80, sodium borate, yeast protein |
| Influenza (Afluria) Trivalent/ Quadrivalent | sodium chloride, monobasic sodium phosphate, dibasic sodium phosphate, monobasic potassium phosphate, potassium chloride, calcium chloride, sodium taurodeoxycholate, ovalbumin, sucrose, neomycin sulfate, polymyxin B, beta- |

| | |
|---|---|
| | propiolactone, thimerosal (multi-dose vials) |
| Influenza (Fluad) | squalene, polysorbate 80, sorbitan trioleate, sodium citrate dehydrate, citric acid monohydrate, neomycin, kanamycin, barium, egg proteins, CTAB (cetyltrimethylammonium bromide), formaldehyde |
| Influenza (Fluarix) Trivalent/ Quadrivalent | octoxynol-10 (TRITON X-100), α-tocopheryl hydrogen succinate, polysorbate 80 (Tween 80), hydrocortisone, gentamicin sulfate, ovalbumin, formaldehyde, sodium deoxycholate, sodium phosphate-buffered isotonic sodium chloride |
| Influenza (Flublok) Trivalent/Quadrivalent | sodium chloride, monobasic sodium phosphate, dibasic sodium phosphate, polysorbate 20 (Tween 20), baculovirus and *Spodoptera frugiperda* cell proteins, baculovirus |

## CDC Excipient Table

| | |
|---|---|
| | and cellular DNA, Triton X-100, lipids, vitamins, amino acids, mineral salts |
| Influenza (Flucelvax) Trivalent/Quadrivalent | Madin Darby Canine Kidney (MDCK) cell protein, protein other than HA, MDCK cell DNA, polysorbate 80, cetyltrimethlyammonium bromide, and β-propiolactone |
| Influenza (Flulaval) Trivalent/Quadrivalent | ovalbumin, formaldehyde, sodium deoxycholate, α-tocopheryl hydrogen succinate, polysorbate 80, thimerosal (multi-dose vials) |
| Influenza (Fluvirin) | ovalbumin, polymyxin, neomycin, betapropiolactone, nonylphenol ethoxylate, thimerosal |
| Influenza (Fluzone) Quadrivalent | egg protein, octylphenol ethoxylate (Triton X-100), sodium phosphate-buffered isotonic sodium chloride solution, thimerosal (multi-dose vials), sucrose |

| | |
|---|---|
| Influenza (Fluzone) High Dose | egg protein, octylphenol ethoxylate (Triton X-100), sodium phosphate-buffered isotonic sodium chloride solution, formaldehyde, sucrose |
| Influenza (Fluzone) Intradermal | egg protein, octylphenol ethoxylate (Triton X-100), sodium phosphate-buffered isotonic sodium chloride solution, sucrose |
| Influenza (FluMist) Quadrivalent | monosodium glutamate, hydrolyzed porcine gelatin, arginine, sucrose, dibasic potassium phosphate, monobasic potassiumphosphate, ovalbumin, gentamicinsulfate, (EDTA), ethylenediaminetetraacetic acid |
| Japanese Encephalitis (Ixiaro) | aluminum hydroxide, protamine sulfate, formaldehyde, bovine serum |

## CDC Excipient Table

| | |
|---|---|
| | albumin, host cell DNA, sodium metabisulphite, host cell protein |
| Meningococcal (MenACWY-Menactra) | Watson Scherp media containing casamino acid modified culture medium containing hydrolyzed casein ammonium sulfate sodium phosphate formaldehyde, sodium chloride |
| Meningococcal (MenACWY-Menveo) | formaldehyde, amino acids, yeast extract, Franz complete medium, CY medium |
| Meningococcal (MPSV4-Menomune) | Mueller Hinton casein agar, Watson Scherp casamino acid media, thimerosal (multi-dose vials), lactose |
| Meningococcal (MenB–Bexsero) | aluminum hydro E. coli, histi sucrose, deoxycho |

| | |
|---|---|
| | kanamycin |
| Meningococcal (MenB - Trumenba) | defined fermentation growth media, polysorbate 80, histidine buffered saline. |
| MMR (MMR-II) | chick embryo cell culture, WI-38 human diploid lung fibroblasts, vitamins, amino acids, fetal bovine serum, sucrose, glutamate, recombinant human albumin, neomycin, sorbitol, hydrolyzed gelatin, sodium phosphate, sodium chloride |
| MMRV (ProQuad) (Frozen) | chick embryo cell culture, WI-38 human diploid lung fibroblasts MRC-5 cells, sucrose, hydrolyzed gelatin, sodium chloride, sorbitol, monosodium L-glutamate, sodium phosphate dibasic, human albumin, sodium bicarbonate, potassium phosphate monobasic, potassium chloride; potassium phosphate dibasic, neomycin, bovine calf serum |
| MMRV (ProQuad) (Refrigerator Stable) | chick embryo cell culture, WI-38 human diploid lung |

| | |
|---|---|
| | fibroblasts, MRC-5 cells, sucrose, hydrolyzed gelatin, urea, sodium chloride, sorbitol, monosodium L-glutamate, sodium phosphate, recombinant human albumin, sodium bicarbonate, potassium phosphate potassium chloride, neomycin, bovine serum albumin |
| Pneumococcal (PCV13 – Prevnar 13) | soy peptone broth, casamino acids and yeast extract-based medium, CRM197 carrier protein, polysorbate 80, succinate buffer, aluminum phosphate |
| Pneumococcal (PPSV-23 – Pneumovax) | phenol |
| Polio (IPV – Ipol) | Eagle MEM modified medium, calf bovine serum, M-199 without calf bovine serum, vero cells (a continuous line of monkey kidney cells), phenoxyethanol, formaldehyde, neomycin, streptomycin, polymyxin B |
| Rabies (Imovax) | human albumin, neomycin sulfate, phenol red |

| | |
|---|---|
| | indicator, MRC-5 human diploid cells, beta-propriolactone |
| Rabies (RabAvert) | chicken fibroblasts, β-propiolactone, polygeline (processed bovine gelatin), human serum albumin, bovine serum, potassium glutamate, sodium EDTA, ovalbumin neomycin, chlortetracycline, amphotericin B |
| Rotavirus (RotaTeq) | sucrose, sodium citrate, sodium phosphate monobasic monohydrate, sodium hydroxide, polysorbate 80, cell culture media, fetal bovine serum, vero cells *[DNA from porcine circoviruses (PCV) 1 and 2 has been detected in RotaTeq. PCV-1 and PCV-2 are not known to cause disease in humans.]* |
| Rotavirus (Rotarix) | amino acids, dextran, Dulbecco's Modified Eagle Medium (sodium chloride, potassium chloride, magnesium sulfate, ferric (III) nitrate, sodium phosphate, sodium pyruvate, D-glucose, |

| | |
|---|---|
| | concentrated vitamin solution, L-cystine, L-tyrosine, amino acids solution, L-250 glutamine, calcium chloride, sodium hydrogenocarbonate, and phenol red), sorbitol, sucrose, calcium carbonate, sterile water, xanthan *[Porcine circovirus type 1 (PCV-1) is present in Rotarix. PCV-1 is not known to cause disease in humans.]* |
| Smallpox (Vaccinia– ACAM2000) | African Green Monkey kidney (Vero) cells, HEPES, human serum albumin, sodium chloride, neomycin, polymyxin B, Glycerin, phenol |
| Td (Tenivac) | aluminum phosphate, formaldehyde, modified Mueller-Miller casamino acid medium without beef heart infusion, ammonium sulfate |
| Td (Mass Biologics) | aluminum phosphate, formaldehyde, thimerosal, modified Mueller's media which contains bovine extracts, ammonium sulfate |

| | |
|---|---|
| Tdap (Adacel) | aluminum phosphate, formaldehyde, 2-phenoxyethanol, Stainer-Scholte medium, casamino acids, dimethyl-beta-cyclodextrin, glutaraldehyde, modified Mueller-Miller casamino acid medium without beef heart infusion, ammonium sulfate, modified Mueller's growth medium |
| Tdap (Boostrix) | modified Latham medium derived from bovine casein, Fenton medium containing a bovine extract, formaldehyde, modified Stainer-Scholte liquid medium, glutaraldehyde, aluminum hydroxide, sodium chloride, polysorbate 80 |
| Typhoid (inactivated – Typhim Vi) | Hexadecyltrimethyl-ammonium bromide, formaldehyde, phenol, polydimethylsiloxane, disodium phosphate, monosodium phosphate, semi-synthetic medium |
| Typhoid (Vivotif Ty21a) | yeast extract, casein, dextrose, galactose, sucrose, ascorbic acid, amino acids, lactose, magnesium stearate. gelatin |

## CDC Excipient Table

| | |
|---|---|
| Varicella (Varivax) *Frozen* | human embryonic lung cell cultures, guinea pig cell cultures, human diploid cell cultures (WI-38), human diploid cell cultures (MRC-5), sucrose, hydrolyzed gelatin, sodium chloride, monosodium L-glutamate, sodium phosphate dibasic, potassium phosphate monobasic, potassium chloride, EDTA (Ethylenediaminetetraacetic acid), neomycin, fetal bovine serum |
| Varicella (Varivax) *Refrigerator Stable* | human embryonic lung cell cultures, guinea pig cell cultures, human diploid cell cultures (WI-38), human diploid cell cultures (MRC-5), sucrose, hydrolyzed gelatin, urea, sodium chloride, monosodium L-glutamate, sodium phosphate dibasic, potassium phosphate monobasic, potassium chloride, neomycin, bovine calf serum |
| Yellow Fever (YF- Vax) | sorbitol, gelatin, sodium chloride, egg protein |
| Zoster (Shingles – Zostavax) *Frozen* | sucrose, hydrolyzed porcine gelatin, sodium chloride, monosodium L-glutamate, |

| | |
|---|---|
| | sodium phosphate dibasic, potassium phosphate monobasic, potassium chloride; MRC-5 cells, neomycin, bovine calf serum |
| Zoster (Shingles – Zostavax)<br>*Refrigerator Stable* | sucrose, hydrolyzed porcine gelatin, urea, sodium chloride, monosodium L-glutamate, sodium phosphate dibasic, potassium phosphate monobasic, potassium chloride, MRC-5 cells, neomycin, bovine calf serum |

A table listing vaccine excipients and media *by excipient* can be found in:
Grabenstein JD. *ImmunoFacts: Vaccines and Immunologic Drugs* – 2013 (38th revision). St Louis, MO: Wolters Kluwer Health, 2012.

# Acknowledgements

In 2015, I visited an old friend who now lives in Costa Rica. I discovered he and his wife were parenting an autistic daughter. After listening to the tragic events of their story, I knew I had to look into the vaccine issue to find out the real implication behind the medical establishment's claim that all vaccines are safe and effective. That led to the research which eventually became the foundation for this book.

I need to recognize the inspiration I received from the following people, without whom this book would not have been possible.

Barbara Loe Fisher, as co-founder of the National Vaccine Information Center, was instrumental in swaying the Health Act of 1986 towards children's rights. Thank you, Barbara.

Robert F. Kennedy, Jr., the environmental attorney who originally fought against industrial dumping of contaminants like mercury, who then took up the fight to eliminate mercury in children's vaccines, and who remains an inspiration for all of us to fight for what's right.

Dr. Sherri Tenpenny is foremost among the researchers who uncovered the fact that nobody knew the cause of death of smallpox.

Dr. Suzanne Humphies challenged conventional wisdom by showing that smallpox was eradicated by improved sanitation and hygiene measures, not by a smallpox vaccine.

Del Bigtree, who produced the long-running daytime television series, "The Doctors," as well as speaking out about vaccine cover-ups in the documentary film: "Vaxxed – From Cover-up to Catastrophe," has an internet show called High Wire where he exposes the false claims of Big Pharma and its minions.

The film, Vaxxed, documents the cover-up of vaccine-injured children by health care providers, and how it was exposed by a scientist who could no longer "play the game." Dr. William Thompson had to "come clean" to assuage his guilt for being part of denying that the autism epidemic was caused by vaccines. Viewers got an inside look at the hidden practices of the pharmaceutical industry, the medical authorities who support the vaccines and drugs, and the cover-up that ensues to discredit anyone who dares to tell the truth.

Due to premiere at New York City's Tribeca Film Festival in 2016, the film was forced to withdraw because of tremendous pressure from various factions. This forced withdrawal of a documentary film was the sign that our freedom of speech was in jeopardy.

Other films began to manifest from other people who experienced vaccine injuries, either directly or indirectly. Soon, it became obvious that an entire movement of people had been harmed by vaccines, and they wanted their version of vaccine safety to become public knowledge.

I came to the realization that the vaccine story was not a simple narrative between pro and con groups. The more I delved into the intricate motives behind the statements and actions of so-called government regulatory bodies, my research developed into a Sherlock Holmes detective mystery to determine the real culprits behind today's autism epidemic.

A major discovery was that anti-vaccine groups were mostly generated by mothers who were pestered by pediatricians and doctors to vaccinate their kids against their own better judgment, and subsequently saw a healthy child regress into autism. Although the medical industry denies that vaccines cause autism, the fact remains that autism always shows up after vaccination, never before.

On a Facebook group for authors, I found an old friend, Joan Murphy, who said she was interested in the theme of my book and would give it a read. It turned out that she was quite a competent editor and thus the book was improved immensely by her guidance.

Now that I had a manuscript that was logical, scientific, and portrayed in an understandable way for the general public, I was ready to publish.

Of course, I must also give immense credit to my beautiful young wife, Chris, who encouraged me along the way, even when the going got tough and it looked like I was on a wild goose chase through a labyrinth of tunnels with no light at the end.

# About the Author

Bestselling author and Investigative Journalist, Pierre St. Clair, digs behind the headlines of today's news to give you the real story beyond the hype.

In 2015 he won the prestigious Sir J. C. Bose Award for Investigative Journalism in the field of Science and Technology for his book *Cosmology on Trial.*

Although born in London, at five years of age his family emigrated to Canada. His mother was a cultured lady who sent him for violin and music theory lessons when he was only six. As a teenager his interest in classical violin dwindled. He bought his first guitar, taught himself how to play, formed a band, and began performing locally.

Within a few short years he was touring throughout Canada and the US. Music was his first love and remains so.

His journalism career began partially as a result of his college girlfriend's mother. The daughter of a missionary in Shanghai, she had grown up in China and pursued an interest in the occult sciences, including palmistry. One Saturday afternoon she asked to see his hand.

"After a few minutes study, she told me that I had a talent for writing. She said, 'One day you will become an author.' Soon that writing talent began to manifest itself.

"My interest in writing, and especially research, continued to increase. I loved digging behind the scenes to find out what was really happening beneath the headlines. That's how I became an investigative journalist.

"I've traveled to 76 countries in the course of investigating a variety of stories. Travel has been my best education about culture, tradition, and food. Yes, I also have a gourmet lifestyle dining on an assortment of traditional cuisines worldwide."

Please visit his Author Page:

http://www.amazon.com/author/pierrestclair

# One Last Thing

If you're reading this, it means you purchased my book and have read it.

My heartfelt thanks for your support.

So, what did you think? If you liked the book, found it useful, enlightening, entertaining, or have something to say, let me know what you liked, or what you thought was lacking, by posting a short review on Amazon.

It doesn't have to be glowing, just your honest experience. When you share your comments, it gives potential readers an idea of the book's value.

Here is the URL for readers in the USA:

https://www.amazon.com/create-review/B077NX99G9#

Amazon will ask you to sign in, and then take you directly to the review page where you can click on one of the stars to post your review.

If you do not live in the USA, you can post your review by clicking the review link on the same Amazon page where you purchased this book.

Thank you,

Pierre St Clair

# Endnotes

[1] T. Obukhanych, *Vaccine Illusion*,

[2] Interview with Dr. Blaylock, *The Truth About Vaccines*, documentary by Ty Bollinger

[3] Interview with Dr. Palevsky, *The Truth About Vaccines*, documentary by Ty Bollinger

[4] Interview with Dr. Tenpenny, *Vaccines Revealed*, documentary by Dr. Patrick Gentempo

[5] T. Obukhanych, *Vaccine Illusion*,

[6] CBS television interview

[7] CBS television interview

[8] Interview with Dr. Thomas, *The Truth About Vaccines*, documentary by Ty Bollinger

[9] https://www.cdc.gov/ncbddd/autism/data.html

[10] http://info.cmsri.org/vaccinated-vs.-unvaccinated/

[11] http://www.viewbix.com/v/Unvaccinated-Children-Healthier/a75dae69-a6e2-478b-a4ac-708545b36725

[12] http://healthimpactnews.com/2011/new-study-vaccinated-children-have-more-diseases-and-disorders/

[13] http://www.vaccineinjury.info/survey/results-unvaccinated/results-illnesses.html

[14] Interview with Barbara Loe Fisher, *Vaccines Revealed*, documentary by Dr. Patrick Gentempo

[15] Interview with Barbara Loe Fisher, *Vaccines Revealed*, documentary by Dr. Patrick Gentempo

[16] http://www.nvic.org/injury-compensation.aspxe

Made in the USA
Lexington, KY
01 August 2018